UN-BREAK-ABLE

by
Kevin Marius

Copyright © 2023 by Kevin Marius
All rights reserved. Published by

Blue Café Books *for*
www.carladupont.com
Atlanta, GA
Printed in the USA.
ISBN: 979-8-218-32520-6

All rights reserved. In accordance with the U.S. Copyright Act of 1976, the scanning, uploading, and electronic sharing of any part of this book without the permission of the publisher constitutes unlawful piracy and theft of the author's intellectual property. If you would like to use material from the book (other than for review purposes), prior written permission must be obtained by contacting Kevin Marius at info@kevinmarius.com.
Thank you for supporting the author's rights.

Credits
Editorial: Carla DuPont
Cover Design: Garrett Myers

DEDICATION

Before dedicating this book, I humbly express my gratitude to God for granting me the opportunity to write and share these stories. Through His guidance and blessings, I have found the strength to overcome life's trials and now extend a helping hand to you, dear reader.

With heartfelt appreciation, I dedicate this book to my wife, Tabitha Marius, our two precious daughters, my family, and in memory of my dad. Your unwavering support, love, and understanding have been the driving force behind my pursuit of resilience and success. You have been my constant pillars of strength, inspiring me to keep pushing forward and reminding me of the importance of family throughout this journey.

To my cherished friends and extended family, your meaningful support and belief in me have been instrumental in my ability to persevere through life's challenges. Your presence, advice, and uplifting spirit have made the difference on countless occasions. This dedication is a testament to the bonds we have forged and the strength we derive from our connections.

To my colleagues at Home Depot, thank you for creating an environment that fostered personal and professional growth. Your guidance, mentorship, and belief in my potential have played a significant role in shaping the person I am today. Your camaraderie and encouragement have been invaluable assets in my quest for resilience.

Finally, to you, dear reader. May the contents of this book inspire you, provide solace during difficult times, and equip you with the tools needed to navigate life's arduous paths. May you find solace, guidance, and empowerment within these pages, knowing you are not alone in your struggles. Your willingness to embark on this journey with me fills my heart with gratitude.

With deepest appreciation and love,
Kevin

PREFACE

Welcome to *Unbreakable: How I Turned My Story of Struggle, Resilience, Perseverance, and Grief into Motivation.* This book is a collection of personal stories that encompass various facets of my life. Through these experiences, I aim to inspire and equip you with the necessary tools to navigate the challenges life presents.

Each chapter delves into different aspects of my life, shedding light on the struggles I faced, the resilience I developed, the perseverance I demonstrated, the grief I encountered, and ultimately, the success I achieved. By sharing my story, my intention is to provide you with valuable insights and lessons that can help you overcome obstacles and find the strength to keep moving forward.

Life can be unpredictable and demanding, but it is through these very trials that we discover our inner reservoirs of resilience and fortitude. As you immerse yourself in the pages of this book, my hope is that you will find inspiration and solace knowing you are not alone in your struggles. Through my experiences, I aim to instill within you a sense of hope, aspiration, and the courage to face life's challenges head-on.

Remember, this book is not just about me; it is an invitation for you to start on your own personal voyage of growth and self-discovery. Together, let us navigate the complexities of life, armed with the wisdom gained from overcoming adversity. May this book serve as a guiding light, illuminating the path towards a life filled with fulfillment and triumph.

My scars bear witness to a story, a testament to moments when life attempted to shatter my spirit but ultimately faltered. They serve as indelible markers, revealing where the framework of my character was forged.

There comes a time when all that remains is to fight, to summon every ounce of strength within and rise once more. In those moments, one word encompasses it all: "resilience." This single word carries profound significance.

PREFACE

Resilience, the capacity to swiftly recover from hardships, embodies the ability to withstand adversity and rebound from life's most challenging trials. It is defiance in the face of setbacks, defying the notion of being broken.

For within resilience lies the essence of being unbreakable. It is the embodiment of a spirit that refuses to yield, a force that persists despite the odds. It is the steadfast resolve to navigate the storms of life and emerge stronger on the other side.

In the depths of my being, I carry a story of resilience, a tale of transformation that has shaped the person I am today. Scars, both visible and hidden, bear witness to the trials and tribulations I have faced. Each scar tells a chapter, a moment in time where life tested my spirit, yet failed to break me.

In the face of adversity, I made a choice. I chose to rise above the darkness and rebuild my shattered world. It was not an easy path, for it demanded courage, resilience, and a willingness to confront my deepest fears. With each step forward, I discovered a reservoir of inner strength I never knew existed.

There were moments when the journey seemed unbearable, when doubt and self-doubt threatened to undermine my progress. In those moments, I called upon the lessons of endurance learned along the way. I reminded myself scars do not define weakness; rather, they serve as badges of honor, proof of my endurance and ability to overcome.

Through the process of healing, I discovered the power of self-reflection and self-care. I learned to listen to the whispers of my heart and to prioritize my own well-being. I surrounded myself with a supportive network of loved ones who lifted me up when I faltered. Together, we navigated the twists and turns of this arduous journey, providing solace, understanding, and a steady hand to guide me forward.

May my story inspire others who are facing their own trials, reminding them that within the depths of their struggles lies the potential for transformation. Let them find solace in the knowledge that scars do not equate to weakness, but rather to the indomitable spirit that resides within us all.

In sharing, I hope to ignite a glint of hope in those who need it most. May they discover their own resilience, embrace their scars, and find the courage to forge ahead, knowing that they, too, can emerge unbreakable...something that cannot be broken or shattered. The term conveys a sense of durability, resilience, or steadfastness.

> *"The human spirit is unbreakable, for it finds its greatest strength in the face of adversity."*
> *- Unknown*

Thank you for taking this ride with me. May you find the inspiration and strength within these pages to continue moving forward, unbreakable and undeterred, ready to embrace the limitless possibilities that await you.

Wishing you a transformative and empowering reading experience.

CONTENTS

ONE: The Journey to a New Land 1

TWO: Embracing Resilience and Realizing Dreams 20

THREE: From Struggle to Triumph 39

FOUR: Grief and Heartbreak 52

FIVE: Hitting Rock Bottom 68

SIX: A Journey of Self-Discovery and Success 87

SEVEN: From Challenges to Triumph 106

EIGHT: Overcoming Obstacles to Start a Family 128

NINE: Gratitude and Reflection 142

TEN: Six Steps to Change Your Circumstances and Become *UNBREAKABLE* 154

UN-
BREAK
ABLE

CHAPTER 1

The Journey to a New Land

Saying Goodbye to the Familiar and Stepping into the Unknown

Having spent my formative years in a modest dwelling, home became the center of my world. Although I took my first breath in the United States, it was in the vibrant nation of Haiti that I spent my formative years. The amazing mornings began with the sweet smell of coffee brewing and the familiar sound of roosters crowing, gently waking me up. The warm morning shower added to the comforting start, creating a sensory experience that captured the essence of the day.

There, in a tiny apartment in Petion-Ville, a commune and suburb of Port-au-Prince, Capital of Haiti, my parents rented their first apartment after getting married. The apartment was essentially a long hallway with various compartments. My parents transformed the dining room into both a bedroom and dining space. It was in this area that my sister and I shared a bed, cherishing the closeness it fostered.

In a country where access to electricity is limited to just 40 percent of the population and natural gas is a luxury beyond reach, our appliances served a different purpose.

They became mere fixtures, adorned with roaches and piled with old books, symbolizing our resourcefulness in the face of scarcity. Despite our limited financial means, we embraced the philosophy of making the most out of what we had.

Our cooking area was located outside near the back door, where a rocket stove and a large piece of burning wood and charcoal were our tools. My parents hired a lady to assist us, the agreement was simple: a reasonable sum of money along with a place to stay. As far back as I can recall, she spent the majority of her time in the kitchen. With limited space in the apartment, the kitchen also served as her bedroom.

She worked hard to make sure our breakfasts were ready. She put a lot of effort into making our mornings special. I remember the way her cooking filled our home with the most amazing smells. She knew exactly what she was doing. The sound of food sizzling in the pan and steam rising from the pots were like a signal that a new day was starting.

You know what made her presence even more special? The way she made our mornings feel. We'd all sit together at the table, a palpable warmth spreading. We'd talk and laugh and share stories. It felt like we were all close, like a family. Breakfast wasn't just about eating – it was a tradition that started our day with happiness. Looking back, I'm so thankful for the something special she added becoming part of our family.

Over the years, we grew very close. She patiently taught me to cook, step-by-step, with the belief that one day I would be able to fend for myself. Additionally, she guided me on how to wash, iron, and fold my clothes. The skills she imparted ultimately played a crucial role during my survival mode, helping me navigate life's difficulties with resilience and self-sufficiency.

I assisted her preparing spices, utilizing a pilon, an essential utensil found in most Haitian kitchens, to smash seasonings and crushing them to season the meat. As a special treat, she would save extra pieces of chicken for me as she cooked. Our connection deepened over the years. Despite not having her own children, she found a son in me, and I found a mother in her.

On weekends, my parents would hire this man, well known in the community, to transport water from the fountain down the hill to our home, filling up a large metal barrel in the kitchen. Above it, plywood served as the kitchen countertop. We had to be mindful of our water use to save money. Another option for water was placing a barrel outside to collect rainwater, which we used for showering and washing clothes. The barrel in the kitchen was reserved for food and beverages.

On Saturday evenings, my mom reviewed Bible verses with us, rehearsing for Sunday school service. I loved the Bible. I even took part in preaching during small gatherings, and at home. During school vacation, having a daily church service at noon was a must for us, a tradition upheld by my mother. My sister sang, and I delivered the sermon. I was deeply passionate about it, to the extent that I gained a new nickname in the neighborhood. They called me "Little Pastor." My dad teased me, but he was genuinely impressed by my ability to understand the gospel at such a young age. I began doing this when I was just

6 years old. Through these early Bible studies, we were taught core values. The Bible served as a source of moral and ethical guidance for us. Its stories, teachings, and principles imparted important values like love, compassion, honesty, humility, and the significance of treating others with kindness and respect. These values lay the foundation for our moral and ethical development. On certain evenings, my mother would gather us to tell stories as we gazed at the moonlight. Among them was the story of my own birth.

My mother was pregnant during a tumultuous time in 1987, right when the Haitian coup d'état was unfolding, plunging the country into chaos. During this period, my father was enlisted in the Haitian military. Through his service to the nation, he managed to secure a U.S. visa for himself and our family. My father's aspiration was for me to be the family's savior, with the plan for me to be born on American soil, serving as the bridge to obtain their permanent residency. Becoming the family's beacon of hope, all while having no idea what the future held, was a weighty burden I carried right from the start.

I came into this world prematurely, at just eight months, through a harrowing C-section procedure. The doctor presented my mother with a dire ultimatum, warning that both our lives hung in the balance. She had barely disembarked from an airplane and was rushed directly to the hospital as her water broke during the flight.

She was urgently whisked into the surgical room, where I made my entrance on April 23, 1988. A fragile being so small, I was immediately transported to the neonatal intensive care unit (NICU). The doctors and nurses harbored deep concerns about my survival, uncertain of what the future held. Yet, against all odds, I defied their expectations. This early struggle became a defining testament to my resilience—a resolute indication of the fighter I would grow to become. With each retelling, the story wove itself deeper into my consciousness, shaping my identity and fortifying my determination. The words were more than just sentences; they were the threads that knitted the fabric of my being. I absorbed the core of my mission, realizing difficulties were not burdens but steppingstones, each one designed to enhance my power and improve my spirit.

When my mom returned to Haiti, chaos had become a constant in our lives. From 1988 to 2004, the country experienced four coup d'états, two of them occurring in 1988, the very year I was born. Thus, we never knew true peace. My father consistently dedicated his utmost effort to ensure our safety. He served as a source of motivation and a visionary leader within our family. However, given the state of the country, it was impossible not to worry. We weren't a wealthy family; neither were we poor. We embraced contentment with what we had. My father ensured we lacked nothing by working multiple jobs to provide for his family. This man never ceased to amaze me.

During weekends, television was off the table due to our lack of electricity. Other times when we did have electricity for a brief period, its availability was uncertain. I spent my time flying kites, playing basketball, and riding my bicycle around the neighborhood. I did this before Dad got home. He was a very organized man who thought the house should always be tidy. So, I had to rush home before he arrived to make sure my room was in order.

One vivid memory I have is from the early mornings. As

he prepared to leave for the day in his military uniform, I would be up too, dressed in a miniature version of his attire, complete with a water gun. I aspired to be just like him. I would watch him walk towards the door, and he wouldn't leave until he saluted me, and I saluted him back. That simple exchange brightened my entire day.

Late at night, I became keenly aware of his arrival time. It was my duty to prepare his sandals and clothes, neatly arranging towels for his shower. My endeavors were met with gratification; in the early hours of the morning, he would leave me a few dollars, and I would gleefully use it to indulge in candy or *fritay* (a Haitian term for fried foods). Evening conversations with him became cherished moments, before he settled in for the night, and these exchanges frequently extended for hours.

My dad really believed in the power of education. He did everything he could to get us into prestigious schools in Haiti. We were lucky to attend some of the best private schools in the whole country. He even paid for after-school programs, especially for me because I was the one who had the most trouble in class.

As a hard worker and visionary, his dream was always to better his family's life. One special day, he walked in with a big smile on his face. He had exciting news to tell us – unbelievable and seemingly impossible, we were moving to a new house. He had worked hard and saved money to build a wonderful new home for our family. In this new house, each of us would have our own room, and there was a beautiful backyard to enjoy. We were so happy! Our smiles said it all. It was a moment I'll never forget, a feeling of happiness hard to put into words.

During that period, Haiti was significantly afflicted by political turmoil and instability. My family and I faced unimaginable challenges and lived in constant fear. Our once peaceful country had descended into chaos, with violence and insecurity becoming a daily reality. Just a month before the then President-elect was set to take office, an attempted coup d'état unfolded in the early hours of January 7, 1991. It began with sustained gunfire near the President's Office, prompting an immediate response from the population. People took over the streets, erecting barricades with burning tires throughout the city. Tragically, lives were lost, and multiple individuals were wounded during the violent clashes that erupted in Port-au-Prince.

As the situation escalated, the President was compelled to evacuate the National Palace and was taken to the military headquarters, where he was forced to resign. The initial days of conflict resulted in hundreds of casualties, particularly in the impoverished neighborhoods of the capital. This period was marked by a challenging path through an embargo, rampant insecurity, and ongoing violence.

Years later, the President returned, hoping to bring about peace after a prolonged period of chaos. However, the Haitian military had been disbanded in 1995 due to its involvement in multiple coups and allegations of political interference. Consequently, members of the military were targeted and assassinated by the new regime. It felt like a miracle every time someone left their house and returned safely, given the ongoing instability and uncertainty that gripped the nation during those times.

My father served in the military, and each day brought

news of fellow military members facing danger. Some were tragically assassinated, some in front of their families, some on the streets, and others simply disappeared, never to return home. My father always came home late from work and every time he was extremely late, our hearts filled with worry, fearing the worst. Our anxiety would subside only when he returned home safely. Yet, the cycle of worry would begin anew each time he set out to earn a living in the perilous streets of Haiti. So, we lived in constant fear of losing him to the political unrest that engulfed the country. Yet, his life was spared, and we thanked God for His grace and protection. It was a stark reminder of the fragility of life and the unpredictability of our circumstances.

Haiti also experienced a distressing surge in kidnappings for ransom, which sadly became a common occurrence in people's daily lives, intensifying the existing atmosphere of fear and insecurity. As gang violence escalated, thousands of individuals were forced to flee their homes within the country, illustrating that the danger that loomed was indiscriminate, affecting both adults and children. Every day, as I left for school, my heart would be filled with both hope and trepidation. I prayed for my safe return home and that my family would be untouched by the violence and cruelty plaguing our nation. Stories of break-ins, killings, rape, kidnapping, and robbery circulated within our community as constant reminders of the dangers that lurked just beyond our doorstep.

In, 2004, significant political turmoil set the stage for a tumultuous year. By late February, the President had fled the country, leaving behind a deeply divided nation. This power vacuum resulted in escalating conflicts between his supporters and rivals, leading to hundreds of casualties. Violent riots erupted as a response to the high cost of living, and a substantial portion of the anger was directed towards the government. This further fueled major violence, resulting in more lives being lost.

During this period, gangs began targeting students, kidnapping them for substantial ransoms. If parents were unable to pay, these students often went missing, exacerbating the crisis and deepening the sense of insecurity and instability in the country.

Every day, we faced the daunting task of navigating streets obstructed by barricades and burning tires. It had sadly become a regular occurrence to witness people throwing glass bottles and rocks, and to see the unfortunate aftermath of numerous injuries. On some days, we found ourselves caught in the crossfire as men and police exchanged gunfire, desperately running for cover. With my school bag in tow, I prayed that I would make it to school safely, often arriving late.

Sometimes, to protect ourselves, we had to remove our shirts, concealing the fact that we were on our way to school, and then put on our uniform tops halfway before entering the school premises. The challenges we faced just to get an education were immense, but our determination to learn kept us going.

One day, we set off for school, without a clue what was about to unfold. Out of nowhere, a creepy feeling of danger overtook me. It hit me hard – my life was at risk. Gang members, armed with scary machetes and threatening guns, suddenly appeared, going wild chasing after our vehicle. The atmosphere was a mix of confusion and fear, like a dangerous dance of survival happening right before our eyes. We saw death coming! And this wasn't a one-time thing.

These men aimed to ban school to further their political agenda, and that day, our lives were in grave danger. In the midst of all this chaos caused by the scary gang members chasing us, I turned to prayer for comfort. It was a natural reaction, considering the sad fact that kids caught in such situations often don't make it out okay. Some lose their lives and become examples, while others just disappear without a trace.

And then, at a pivotal moment, our driver turned into a hero. Quick as lightning, he shifted gears, backed up, and made a sharp turn. A brilliant move, using the fact that there were no cars following us. It was like a game of seconds, a dance with fate that got us out of danger's way.

When I think back to that heart-stopping moment, I can't help but believe God was at work. When I returned home that day, I was completely shaken. I had no idea what to do with myself; I felt utterly lost. I just lay in my bed, a kid overwhelmed by thoughts. Would I even get the chance to grow up and discover who I could become? Or would the dangerous streets of Haiti end my life prematurely? Despite the overwhelming challenges and the constant threat to our safety, we held on to hope and resilience. We knew that giving in to fear was not an option; it would only weaken us and prevent us from moving forward. I would return home and attempt to confront these challenges on my own, aspiring to be as strong as my dad.

I learned resiliency from him. He grew up in poverty, studying under the faint light of a streetlamp, the illumination of a full moon, or the glow of a *lanp tet gridap*, a common oil lamp made from recycled cans in Haiti. Often, he went for several days without a proper meal, but his determination to obtain an education burned brightly because he understood it was his only path to a better life. He wore the same clothes for weeks, unable to afford new ones, and lacked the funds to purchase textbooks. To overcome these challenges, he would painstakingly copy lessons from other children's books after school or, when he could spare a few cents, make copies of the required pages.

His father abandoned him at birth, leaving his mother to raise both he and his brother in a humble home constructed from mud and covered with hay. Despite her limited means and with the help of his brother, they did their best to support my father's education. In return, he made a solemn promise to himself: to achieve success and give back to his brother and mother. One of the first things he did upon reaching success was to build a comfortable home for his mother and brother, fulfilling the pledge he had made.

I've witnessed him dedicating himself to studies in order to earn new degrees and enhance his income, all with the aim of giving us the life we had always envisioned. He achieved a law degree, a business administration degree, and even obtained a Spanish teaching certificate, to teach in public schools. He taught at more than five schools in Haiti, with dedication that amazed me.

In the midst of all the chaos, his resilience shone through. He refused to stay home, opting to forge a path forward. He bounced back from his military service and created new opportunities for himself by returning to school and earning several degrees. His unwavering determination is a testament to the remarkable strength of the human spirit.

The fact that he continued to work, even in the face of gunshots and violence, speaks volumes about his commitment to providing for his family. It's a testament to the deep love and responsibility he felt towards those he cared for, and it showcases his incredible courage and resilience in the face of adversity. That should be inspiration for anyone facing challenges, demonstrating that with determination and an unwavering spirit, it's possible to overcome even the most daunting obstacles.

After we were settled in our new home, my father had a remarkable idea. Despite his own struggles to access quality education as a child, he was determined to open a school to provide education to those less fortunate. This time, we believed him without a doubt, because he had a proven track record of turning dreams into reality. Little did we know, my dad was embarking on a journey that transformed our lives. He added two more floors to our home and converted the bottom two floors into a school.

The school he established swiftly rose to become one of the finest in the area. Most of the students excelled in their state exams, a testament to the high-quality education they were receiving. My dad's commitment didn't stop there; he purchased two more plots of land to expand the school, adding a preschool for the youngest learners. He provided top-tier education at an affordable price, ensuring children had access to opportunities they otherwise might not have had.

My father's visionary mindset is a constant source of inspiration for me. I strive each day to follow in his footsteps, learning from his dedication and determination.

CHAPTER 2

Embracing Resilience and Realizing Dreams

A Journey of Family, Education, and Overcoming Fear

It was a struggle for me to get through my teenage years, which were difficult on both levels, personal and academic. Even though I made every effort to pass through the constant pressures, a nagging sensation of not belonging haunted me. My academic journey was far from being a smooth sail – rather, I found myself grappling with the reality of not shining as the brightest star in the classroom. If anything, I gained a reputation as the disrupter, earning me the unfortunate title of being the class's perennial underachiever. Frequently finding myself in detention for disrupting the class or going against the norm, I was often seen as a rule-breaker, consistently violating school policies. This pattern continued, culminating in the demoralizing experience of being held back three times. As a result, I became the subject of my peers' jokes, calling me the "class grandfather." While the majority of my classmates moved on to the next grade, I found myself in the position of having to repeat the class.

My self-esteem took a severe blow due to the hurtful comments of a geometry teacher who declared, "You will never amount to anything in life. In fact, you will repeat this class three times." This happened during a class where I began chatting with my friends instead of paying attention. This was a particularly terrible blow; as the kids laughed, I was embarrassed. Those words reverberated in my head, enveloping me in a darkness of hopelessness that I struggled with alone. My anguish reached a point where I contemplated the unthinkable; the fear of being misunderstood kept me from sharing my pain with anyone.

My parents, who didn't help my journey go more smoothly, added to the stress. Due to my persistent disruptive behavior and underperformance, which had previously led to multiple expulsions and school changes, those around me became increasingly frustrated. One summer, after receiving news that I failed the state exams and had to repeat the class, my dad's frustration made him say things that made me really think. I started to wonder if these were the same thoughts my hero and role model had about me. *Was I a letdown?* This thought stayed with me. I struggled to figure out how I could make him proud. During that summer, I did my best to avoid him and even felt nervous about looking him in the eyes.

Tears became my constant companions that summer, a measure to the intensity of my emotional turmoil. Even the basic pleasures of playing with friends seemed distant, obscured by the heaviness of my unhappiness. Yet, despite the storm within me, no guardian angel appeared on the horizon, and I was left to deal with my sorrow alone.

I felt bad about myself, like a heavy weight pushing me down. It was like this suffocating feeling encompassing me. I couldn't escape the feeling of shame, and it was tough to deal with. On top of that, I found out my friends knew about it, too. Knowing that just made me feel worse.

When the new school term was getting closer, I started feeling worried about seeing my friends again. They had moved on to the next grade, and I was still stuck in the same one. But I had to face my fears.

All of a sudden, something important changed my outlook when I realized I was on my own journey. I made a deliberate choice to ignore all the noisy opinions around me. Instead, I focused on understanding my worth and what special things I could offer to the world. I started working to get past the limits that used to hold me back. This was the start of my real effort to become the best version of myself.

One evening, my parents sat down to discuss my future. My father, deeply concerned about the challenges I was grappling with, made a choice. He felt that a fresh start in a new environment was imperative. Despite the uncertainty of where I would end up, he was resolute in his decision.

My father's determination brought a glimmer of hope amid the difficult times I was experiencing. He recognized that my best opportunity lay in moving to the United States. This decision was driven by the political unrest in our home country and concerns about my performance in an upcoming state exam. Thus, my father initiated the process to facilitate my departure. While I understood the necessity of this new beginning, I couldn't help but feel apprehensive about the unknown challenges relocating would bring.

My parents' decision was concrete. June 25th, 2005, is a date that forever altered the course of my life—an impactful day when I bid farewell to my cherished home, beloved family, and dear friends in Haiti. Due to the escalating political unrest and my academic concerns, my parents made the difficult but necessary decision to send me to the United States to ensure my safety.

Witnessing lifeless bodies strewn across the streets every morning, left there by gang members as a stark reminder and message to the government, was a horrifying experience. The constant need to seek cover from the sound of gunshots, and the grisly sight of dismembered body parts scattered on the ground, left an indelible mark on me. The sight of wounded individuals only intensified the distress. My heart was never at peace in the midst of such violence and chaos. It was a relentless cycle of uncertainty. Going to school became a daily challenge, where we never knew what to expect. Sometimes, while in class, we would hear news that triggered a rush of parents picking up their children early, knowing that the streets were about to become dangerous. In my case, the decision of whether to stay or leave was often left in my hands, as I used to travel to school alone using public transportation.

Heading home after school was a commute filled with apprehension, always hoping to make it back safely amidst the unpredictable and volatile conditions in the streets.

Unfortunately, my school happened to be situated right in the heart of the riots, adding an additional layer of concern to our already anxious situation. Fearing for my safety, my parents felt an urgent need to make a swift change in my life, particularly for my sake as my sister had just graduated and was preparing to attend college in a more secure area away from the chaos.

I recall observing my dad in the living room tirelessly dialing numerous international numbers, seeking someone who would offer me refuge. The full extent of the situation eluded my young mind; yet a sense of happiness enveloped me as I prepared to embark on a journey to the United States of America—a dream cherished by countless Haitians.

After what seemed like an eternity, my parents finally received a phone call from an unfamiliar voice saying, "We will take the boy." Relief washed over my parents, but within me, conflicting emotions stirred. One part of me embraced happiness, while the other side braced itself for the unknown. The mixture of emotions created a bittersweet sensation deep within.

The long-awaited day finally arrived. In an old beat-up sedan my dad borrowed, together with my uncle they dropped me off at the Toussaint Louverture International Airport. My mom and sister stayed home; I could see bittersweet emotions in their eyes as they stood at the main entrance watching the car drive away.

This was an emotional moment for me. Being separated from my family was something I had never envisioned. In their eyes, I saw a fleeting summary of the wonderful moments we had all shared together, like a rush of memories.

As I gazed out of the back window, I watched our house shrink in my line of sight, gradually disappearing behind the trees. It forced me to shift my focus forward, leaving the past behind and starting a new chapter in my life. When we reached the airport, my dad quickly bought me a sandwich to enjoy before my departure. We were in a rush to ensure I didn't miss my flight. This simple meal became our last shared moment before my journey. Climbing the portable stairs, my eyes fixated on them until the plane obstructed my view. A wave of heartbreaking emotions washed over me, etching this moment deeply in my memories. With no grasp of the English language yet, I braced myself for what lay ahead, aware of the challenges awaiting me, but lacking the preparation to fully navigate them.

Life has a way of surprising us, sometimes in ways we least expect. Despite the challenges we faced together as a family and the unbreakable bond we believed we had; life had its plans for each of us individually. In the blink of an eye, our moment of togetherness was shattered, and we found ourselves facing yet another obstacle.

It is often said that nothing lasts forever, and though it is a difficult truth to accept, it is a reality we all must confront at some point in our lives. Change is inevitable, and sometimes it can come unexpectedly, disrupting the very foundation of our existence.

The circumstances that led to our separation were beyond our control. The pain of separation is a deeply profound and heartbreaking experience.

As the day of my departure drew near, a vivid memory from the past suddenly resurfaced in my mind. It was a memory of my sister and me sitting in our living room, diligently learning English words.

Among the handful of words we memorized, three stood out: yes, no, and chicken. I had focused on these particular words because I thought they would come in handy when the flight attendants asked me what I wanted to eat on the plane. This was back when American Airlines still served full-course meals, and I wanted to be prepared for that experience.

As the day approached, I packed up my belongings into a single suitcase. It was a symbol of leaving behind the familiar and venturing into the unknown. With a mixture of anticipation and nervousness, I was ready to begin a new chapter of my life.

The suitcase represented more than just my physical belongings; it held my hopes, dreams, and the courage to face the challenges that lay ahead. It was a tangible reminder of the decision I had made, to embrace the opportunities that awaited me in a foreign land.

With a mixture of excitement and apprehension, I boarded the plane, ready to begin on a path that would shape the course of my life. I had no clue then that this would be just the beginning of a series of adventures, challenges, and personal growth awaiting me. As I fastened my seatbelt and the plane took off, I left behind the familiar sights and sounds of my home country. Not only would this journey shape my linguistic abilities but also my character, perspective on life, and understanding of the world.

The captain announcing our readiness for take-off echoed over the loudspeaker. I gazed out of the window, capturing one final glimpse of the familiar lands that encompassed the only home I had ever known. With a bittersweet sentiment, I bid my farewell to the place that had shaped my existence until that moment.

As the plane soared through the sky, I couldn't help but feel a mixture of nostalgia and excitement for the unknown. The path ahead might have been uncertain, but it was my belief that carrying the lessons learned from my past and holding onto my dreams offered strength to handle whatever challenges awaited me.

Reflection

In the aftermath of a sudden separation, it is natural to feel a mix of emotions—sadness, confusion, and perhaps even anger. We may question why life tests us in such a way, tearing us apart after all we have endured. The truth is, we may never fully understand the reasons behind these twists and turns, and that is a difficult truth to come to terms with.

However, as we traverse new chapters of our lives, it is important to hold on to the lessons and values that guided us through our previous challenges. The resilience, love, and unity we once shared as friends or family can still serve as beacons of light in the midst of uncertainty. Despite physical separation, the memories and bonds we formed remain a part of us, interwoven into the fabric of who we are.

While it may be difficult to envision a future that looks different from what we had imagined, it is crucial to remain open to the possibilities that lie ahead. Life has a way of presenting us with new opportunities and paths, even amidst the most challenging circumstances. It is during these moments of transition and change that we have the opportunity to rediscover ourselves, redefine our purpose, and find new sources of power and toughness.

Navigating the challenges of moving to a new country.

A familiar voice echoed through the loudspeaker; it was the captain announcing our imminent landing. I shifted my gaze to the window to witness the breathtaking spectacle of the country beneath illuminated by a myriad of twinkling lights that bathed the land in an ethereal glow reminiscent of daylight. Although I had previously traveled to New York, this trip held a profound distinction. This time, my purpose was to establish a permanent presence, to call this place my new home.

Stepping out of the baggage claim area, my grip tight on a single suitcase, I caught sight of a stranger holding a sheet of paper bearing the name "KEVIN." This man, a completely unfamiliar face, stood before me, prompting me to summon my courage and take a leap of faith. With determination in my stride, I walked towards him, mustering the words, "I am Kevin," as an introduction. He extended his hand, and I reciprocated the gesture with a firm handshake. I trailed behind him, entering a burgundy church van.

As we drove along, I marveled at the towering buildings and bustling highways, my thoughts consumed by questions of adaptation and the uncertainty of whether I would reunite with my parents. After reaching the parking lot, we made our way towards the building in Coney Island Sea Rise Housings. We opened the lobby door and waited for the elevator to get to the apartment. There, I was introduced to everyone in the house, who welcomed me with open arms; they were happy to have me as part of the family.

They walked me into the room where I was going to sleep, located by the window facing the playground. In that room, packed with four of us, our living situation was challenging: two bunk beds and one closet. I found myself sharing the space with strangers who later became family; the only familiar face was that of my cousin. He'd arrived years before me. As a matter of fact, he was the only reason I ended up living there. As we steered through circumstances together, we formed a special bond of closeness and support.

Our shared experiences in that crowded room became a

part of our journey, shaping us and strengthening our connection. We leaned on each other, finding strengths and companionship amidst the cramped conditions of feeling abandoned. Together, we faced the adversities and unknowns, understanding we had each other's backs along the way.

That night, that room became the place where I laid my head, yearning to awaken from what felt like a surreal dream. I longed to find myself waking up beside my family. However, as my eyes opened the following day, the radiant sun poured its light into the room on the 9th floor. The cheerful sounds of children playing on the nearby playground reached my ears. It struck me that this was not a nightmare; it was my reality now. Whatever lay ahead, I had come to terms with the fact that I would face it alone summoning the strength within to confront the challenges that awaited me.

I will forever feel grateful for the family who took me in. I was a stranger, but they decided to help me and allowed me to live with their family. That family helped me apply for school to ensure I continued my education. The pastor's wife was the one who helped me with my doctor's appointments. As a minor, I needed a guardian. She would stop everything she was doing to ensure my immunization record was up to date for school. I remember her with a metro card, hopping on every public transportation bus to be on time for all our doctor's appointments.

She was an angel in disguise, she cooked meals for all of us and treated me like her own son. Her sons and daughter took me in as their sibling. We had the most enjoyable time together, which sometimes helped me forget about my nightmare. But home will always be where my heart is. Each night, I found myself consumed by longing, dreaming of the possibility of returning home and cherishing more time with my family. It was different for me, I yearned to escape the confines of this unfamiliar reality, desperately wishing to wake up from what felt like a never-ending nightmare.

With each passing morning, the harsh reality settled deeper in. I felt isolated in a world where I seemed ill-prepared. What was I supposed to do? How was I, a mere

17-year-old kid, expected to figure it all out? Who was there to guide me and show me the path through life?

Questions swirled within me as I wondered why this burden had been placed upon my shoulders. What had I done to deserve such circumstances? Despite my attempts to place blame on God, my country, and even my parents, the circumstances remained unchanged. So, I began to shield my emotion, building a wall to never be hurt again. I had to face my fears and learn how to adapt quickly to survive. Not one day has passed without thinking how my life changed so quickly, I only expected things to get worse. I went from playing basketball, riding bicycles, and flying kites in my homeland to a building on the 9th floor far away from home and my family.

As I write these heartfelt words, my emotions overwhelm me and tears well up in my eyes. This event left an indelible mark on my life, forever altering my perspective. The sense of family, once a cherished part of my existence, seemed to slip away. I implore you to cherish every precious moment in life before they become cherished memories.

My message to those who have relocated from their home country to a foreign land is one of encouragement to persist, regardless of the challenges. I understand these may not be the words you're seeking at this moment, but trust me, there is a promising future ahead. I'm acquainted with numerous peers and colleagues who embarked on similar journeys, leaving their homeland at a young age. The overwhelming uncertainty about life's trajectory can be akin to taking a risk, yet it's crucial to maintain resilience and keep progressing. If I managed to overcome these obstacles, you can, too. The emotional burden of detachment should not be underestimated; it can often feel like living a double life. Find your inner strength as you initiate a new path.

CHAPTER 3

From Struggle to Triumph
_____

Navigating A Language Barrier and Building a New Life

Overcoming the difficulties of adapting to a new language and culture from Haiti to the United States of America was a monumental challenge.

The language barrier became one of the first hurdles to overcome. As you know, English was not my native language, and I struggled to communicate effectively. Every conversation was a learning experience, as I navigated unfamiliar words and phrases, often feeling lost and misunderstood. Adapting to a new culture was equally daunting. The customs, traditions, and social norms were unfamiliar to me. I had to figure out different social dynamics, etiquette, and cultural expectations. It took time and effort to understand and embrace the American way of life while also holding on to the values and traditions that shaped me in Haiti.

Through it all, I remained steadfast. I embraced the challenges as opportunities for growth and learning. I sought support from friends and mentors. Their guidance and encouragement helped me find my place in this new culture and build a sense of belonging.

Adapting to a new language and culture would be a lifelong journey. Each step forward brought me closer to fully welcoming the opportunities and experiences that the United States had to offer. Living in the house and playing with the kids on the playground during the summer I first arrived made me question whether I would ever master this language. I felt frustrated.

Another obstacle arose when I entered high school, as I had to resume my education from where I left off in Haiti. The language barrier posed a significant challenge, but I was determined to find a way to make it work, fully aware that this situation would only be temporary. It required me to steer through unfamiliar educational systems and adapt quickly to succeed.

In addition, I experienced a profound culture shock, as the paradise I had envisioned turned out to be a living nightmare. Surrounded by the distressing reality of gun violence and a high crime rate in Coney Island, I witnessed individuals my age being incarcerated. Living in such an environment meant enduring constant peer pressure and influence that stemmed from my surroundings. The profound wisdom imparted by my mother, a woman of unwavering faith, shaped my early years and instilled in me the importance of prioritizing God over human influences. These invaluable teachings became a beacon of light as I maneuvered the challenging environment of Coney Island, plagued by the presence of drugs, crime, and gangs. My unshakeable faith in God served as my saving grace, providing me with steadfast guidance and support along the way.

While attending school and grappling with the process of adaptation, I endured a period of prolonged silence from my parents, spanning several months. Feeling abandoned and overwhelmed, I found myself in dire need of financial support. The circumstances were particularly challenging considering I came to this country with only 40 American dollars given to me by my father. With that meager amount, I had to prioritize purchasing a coat capable of withstanding the approaching winter season. As a 17-year-old, my circumstances made me anything but an ordinary boy. The carefree days of youth had come to an abrupt halt, as the weight of reality settled upon my shoulders.

My new reality was living amidst a group of strangers, faces entirely unfamiliar to me. Each morning, as hunger gnawed at my stomach, embarrassment ate at my soul. Nevertheless, I couldn't bring myself to open the fridge. Instead, I waited for someone else to do it, and when they did, that was my chance to get what I wanted. My life had undergone a profound and abrupt transformation. In stark contrast to the past, where I woke up to a ready-made breakfast, my new reality demanded that I adapt to a vastly different routine. I had to face my fears and start accepting this new world. So, I was forced to leave behind comfort to act like I truly belonged as a part of this new family. It wasn't simple, adjusting to a new home, but the family welcomed me warmly, which made it easier.

I recalled when the pastor and his wife had a routine of cleaning the church on weekends. We all stayed home the entire day, meaning we had to purchase food. While others indulged in purchasing Chinese food, I didn't have enough money for that, so I often didn't have a proper meal. In those times, the kids would share some rice and wings with me, or I'd make noodles. After school, I would go to the mall to window shop, not buying anything because I had no money. I used to borrow clothes from my new brothers since we all wore approximately the same size. Sneaking in to borrow their sneakers often resulted in getting caught. In the beginning, I felt embarrassed, but eventually, we all embraced the idea of borrowing each other's clothing, sneakers, and jackets because we had grown close and bonded like brothers.

During this period, one thought kept running through my mind: If I could work and earn my own money, my situation would get better.

Like my father always said, working brings freedom. I wanted to be able to buy my own food, clothing, and so forth, and not rely on others. So, my hope for survival rested on finding a job. Every weekend, I woke up with determination, put on my best clothes, and walked the busy streets of New York City. I went to all the businesses I could find and asked if they had any job openings.

I had a folder with multiple copies of my resume in hand. I would give them to receptionists or leave them with the security guards at various places. Nobody called me back.

And if they did, I couldn't communicate well because of my language barrier. Still, I didn't give up. I was determined to work.

Year after year, I kept looking for a job, but nothing came through. Each summer passed with disappointment, and I hoped the next year would be better. Finally, in my senior year of high school, I applied for a job, and they called me for an interview. I waited nervously, and unfortunately, it turned out to be a group interview at a workforce agency. I didn't do well at all. I panicked under the pressure because my inability to communicate was a major challenge. I was sweating and silently praying for it to be over.

Because of the language barrier I faced, my employment opportunities were limited. McDonald's became the only place that would give me a chance. Initially, I was assigned the position of a cashier, but my lack of understanding the customers' orders caused me to panic. Sensing my struggle, my supervisor made the decision to transfer me to the drive-through area, hoping for a better fit, but the language barrier persisted. Finally, the supervisor presented me with the last and only option of working as a janitor, which I gladly accepted, recognizing the pressing need for income.

I attended school in the morning and took the afternoon shift at work. To earn extra income, I dedicated my entire Saturdays and Sundays to working overtime. Whenever my classmates came in, I couldn't help but feel the need to hide. The thought of being seen as a janitor by my peers was disheartening. I wished to shield myself from the potential judgment and stigma associated with my job.

I began working for a mere $6 per hour. Despite the modest pay, it made a significant difference in my life. Finally, I had the means to purchase clothes for school, afford food on the weekends, and even enjoy outings with friends. Alongside my job, I remained committed to excelling in school. It often meant staying up late at night to complete homework after work. Still, I managed to graduate early in January. Although I was offered the opportunity to walk down the aisle during the graduation ceremony and attend prom, I couldn't find a purpose in doing so. With my parents absent to witness those milestones, they seemed meaningless. As a result, I chose not to attend prom or the graduation ceremony. I collected my diploma, closed that chapter of my life, and moved forward.

Leaving the role of janitor to become a cashier at a supermarket marked my next achievement—a significant step forward, especially considering I had initially been turned down for this very position. Progress was evident. Now, I found myself confronting my apprehensions. Although each customer interaction at my register seemed daunting, I persevered, deliberately initiating conversations to enhance my English-speaking abilities.

Gradually, I improved, progressing to the point where I evolved into a master trainer. This role involved mentoring new cashiers, a testament to my dedication and growth. As a result of consistently honing my skills, I eventually became the best cashier in the supermarket.

As the Bible advises, "Do not despise the day of small beginnings." Every journey starts somewhere, and it's crucial to bear in mind that your current position is merely a pause, not your final stop. Similar to a train's announcement, "Stay clear of the closing door, please," rest assured that you will reach your destination. Trust in the process. During those days, my true destiny remained unclear to me. However, I was certain that cultivating resilience was paramount, ensuring I remained unbreakable and resolute, refusing to let my circumstances dictate the course of my future.

Breaking through language barriers to connect with others.

Overcoming the language barrier continued to be my primary challenge, as I wondered how I would ever manage to learn this foreign language. The journey proved to be arduous, even with my enrollment in the ESL (English as a Second Language) class in high school. Despite the support provided, mastering the language remained a significant hurdle.

As I mentioned, communicating with others posed a significant challenge for me. It wasn't just about finding a job; it was about overcoming the fear of being judged for my accent. I was often perceived as a quiet person. The truth is, I was simply afraid to speak up, fearing people would ridicule my pronunciation. It became a recurring experience where I had to repeat myself whenever I opened my mouth, which further added to my unease.

Motivated to conquer the English language, I made a firm commitment to my learning journey. I immersed myself in various activities to enhance my skills. Reading became a regular habit, while watching YouTube videos provided valuable listening practice. Determined to expand my vocabulary, I diligently took notes on new words and phrases. Despite the potential for ridicule, I pushed myself to engage in conversations with friends, gradually building my confidence. I understood that facing laughter or mockery was a small price to pay for the vital progress I was making in mastering English.

Being a Black man in Coney Island projects meant facing the harsh realities of prison, drugs, and gang violence.

The prevailing narrative suggested that having a child at a young age and facing incarceration was destined to be my fate. But I defied the odds and proudly graduated from high school. I also took the bold step of applying to college, charting my own path forward. The journey was far from easy, as I balanced daytime work with evening college classes that often extended into late hours, followed by train rides home.

I can vividly recall days when I was so tired, I'd fall asleep on the train, missing my stop and have to take another ride back home. It was a risky voyage; with a price I was willing to pay to achieve something in life. I didn't want to follow the same path as everyone around me or become just another statistic in America. I aimed to be a role model for others.

I gave up the usual fun that young people have and focused only on my future goals. I wanted to make a unique name for myself. Even though it was tough, I didn't have enough money, and I couldn't get financial aid because of missing paperwork from my parents. The alternative? Paying for my classes one-by-one from my own pocket.

This often made me tight on money, but the feeling of having a clear purpose and making progress made it all worthwhile. Life has a peculiar way of pushing us to our limits, but it also has the power to stretch us beyond our expectations, fostering personal growth and resilience.

As you are reading this, remember there are no quick shortcuts in life. We must go through the journey, overcome challenges, and set an example for others. Strive to make a positive impact on your family and your surroundings. Take actions that your future self will look back on with pride. Success doesn't come easy; you can't skip ahead. Instead, you must climb the stairs, one step at a time. There is no elevator!

CHAPTER 4

Grief and Heartbreak

Navigating Loss and Moving Forward from Afar

Since 2005, when I first left Haiti, I had been angry at my parents for never contacting me. I felt abandoned. Despite my deep-felt emotion, I mustered the courage to call my father on December 31st, 2009. The desire to reach out tugged at my heart during the Christmas season; my lingering anger had held me back. Memories flooded my mind of how our family used to celebrate Christmas together. I recalled my father waking up early, filling the house with the melodies of festive Christmas music—the sound system reserved solely for this special occasion.

"Chantons La Noël" is a song by my dad's favorite group, Tropicana. This song holds a significant place in my memories, as it has been etched into my heart and mind. Whenever I hear the familiar melody and lyrics, it instantly takes me back to cherished moments spent with my dad, singing and dancing together. The rhythm and energy of the song create an atmosphere of joy and celebration, reminding me of the bond we shared. This song has become a nostalgic treasure, symbolizing the love and connection I have with my dad.

Everyone would be hard at work in the kitchen, preparing a delicious feast. The joyous atmosphere was infectious, uniting us all. We would come together around the table, sharing a meal as a family. Later that night, we would eagerly head to church, returning home swiftly to rest, knowing that the morning would bring gifts nestled at our feet.

There was nothing quite like Christmas morning—the anticipation, the excitement, the sheer delight of unwrapping our carefully chosen presents. My sister and I would burst with joy as we revealed the treasures hidden within the wrapping paper. Those memories held a special place in my heart, reminding me of the beauty and unity that Christmas brought to our family.

However, those cherished memories had faded into the past, overshadowed by the years I spent in solitude, detached from it all. But now, I stood at the precipice of change, determined to break free from the walls that confined me. With trembling hands, I grasped the phone and dialed my father's number.

"Hi Dad, it's me. Happy New Year," I uttered, my voice carrying a mix of apprehension and hope. The sheer delight in his response was palpable as he quickly summoned the family, gathering them around the speakerphone to listen to my words. There was a longing within me to inquire why they had not extended a hand, why they had abandoned me. With no calls, no financial assistance, and no visits to bridge the distance between us, I made a conscious choice to embrace the present moment and find solace in the joy it brought.

As the clock ticked past midnight and the New Year began its reign, I shared heartfelt New Year's wishes with each family member. The time flew by, seamlessly transitioning from midnight to the early hours of the morning. In those precious hours, I poured out my emotions, confessing how much I had missed them all.

The conversation stretched on for hours, as we laughed, reminisced, and caught up on the countless moments we had missed. Among words exchanged, I made a promise to my father—one that filled my heart with determination and longing. "Dad, I've missed you. In fact, I've missed all of you. I promise I will come to see you this summer."

In that moment, a renewed sense of hope and connection began to blossom. The darkness that had cloaked my heart for so long started to dissipate, replaced by the flickering light of reconciliation. Hanging up the phone after our conversation, longing washed over me. The vision of being together again, basking in the familiar comforts of family, ignited a fire within me. It was the first step on a journey to reunite with my family and rebuild the bonds that had been lost in the passage of time.

A surge of excitement pulsed through me as I prepared to reunite with my parents, eager to show them how much I had transformed since the days of being a 17-year-old boy in Haiti. The fullness of my beard served as a testament to the passage of time and the growth I'd experienced.

Through careful saving and hard work, I accumulated a sum of money, not much, determined to shower my parents with the spoils they deserved. It was my chance to finally say, "Dad, I've got you," acknowledging and repaying him for the countless years he supported our family financially. The anticipation of this grand gesture filled me with joy. I was ready to return to my homeland and reunite with my friends.

As summer approached, my heart filled with enthusiasm. Each day, I longed more to reunite with my family. The memories of our shared experiences were like hidden treasures, waiting to be rediscovered and cherished again. I yearned to sit around our familiar table, where laughter and love were at the center. My father's jokes used to fill the room, and my sister and I would laugh uncontrollably. The delicious scents of the lady who cooked for us for years would waft through the air, adding to the warmth and enjoyment of the occasion.

The summer offered the hope of bringing back those cherished memories and creating new ones to stay with us forever. The idea of sitting at that table again, surrounded by the contagious joy and love that united us, filled my heart with an indescribable longing.

I eagerly counted down the days, knowing the moment of reunion would be a testament to our unbreakable bond. I longed to express my gratitude and love, to let my parents know just how much their unwavering support meant to me. With every passing moment, I grew more excited to unveil the man I had become, to share my accomplishments and aspirations with those who had nurtured me from the beginning.

On January 12th, a Tuesday, I went out early to do some shopping at the mall, which was my routine on my days off. While on the subway in Manhattan, I lost signal, preventing me from receiving any phone calls or text messages until I got off at one of the stations, by which time it was already 5 p.m. That's when my cousin called me and asked if I had heard what happened in Haiti. I told him no. Then he said, "Check on your family. An earthquake hit Haiti."

Initially, I didn't think it was a big deal because Haiti had experienced smaller earthquakes in the past that weren't catastrophic. So, I didn't give it much thought and told myself I would check as soon as I got home, But then, I received a news update as soon as I got out of the train station stating that a 7.0 magnitude earthquake had struck Haiti, the worst ever recorded, and the death toll was rising rapidly.

As the news of this cataclysmic event reached my eyes, a surge of disbelief and anguish coursed through my veins compelling me to take immediate action. With a sense of urgency, I hastily made my way to the nearest corner store, determined to purchase a calling card that would grant me the opportunity to reach out to my family, seeking reassurance amidst the chaos.

My phone kept buzzing with messages, and everyone was asking the same question: 'Did you hear about what happened in Haiti?' I felt a rush of fear and unease. The truth was, I didn't have any real information yet. I couldn't help myself; I had to know more. I turned to the internet, hoping against hope that the news was wrong or blown out of proportion, seeking some comfort in that possibility.

Sadly, reality hit me hard. As I searched online, I found out the terrible truth: Haiti had been hit by a massive earthquake. It caused terrible destruction and left people in deep despair. My heart ached as I tried to grasp the enormity of the tragedy that struck my homeland.

With a shaky hand and a heavy heart, I dialed the numbers to reach my family. I desperately hoped that they were safe from the worst of the disaster. When my mother's voice finally came through, it was filled with a mix of relief and pain. She shared the devastating news – we had lost my dear father, and my sister was trapped under the rubble, her life hanging by a thread. The gravity of the situation weighed on us as my mother described the terrifying earthquake and the danger they were in.

At that moment, I couldn't believe what I was hearing. I held on to a tiny bit of hope, wondering if maybe my mother had misunderstood or was too scared to give accurate information. I didn't want to accept the heartbreaking truth. Denial became my safehaven, protecting me from the overwhelming pain that was ready to crush my spirit.

I went home, climbed onto my bunk bed, laid my head on

the pillow, and cried for days. I didn't want to leave the room, even though people were trying to comfort me. I was in deep pain and didn't have the appetite to eat. I kept searching the internet and tried calling my family repeatedly, but it was difficult to reach them internationally because of the damage to multiple communication towers. I persisted, even though I could only hear bits of their voices in and out with the signal constantly dropping. I felt helpless because I couldn't be there with my family when they needed me the most. Even in those tough times, a small spark of strength started to grow inside me. I made up my mind to be a source of support for my loved ones, even though we were far apart. I refused to let despair put out the hope burning within all of us.

I couldn't believe what had happened to my homeland. I never imagined it could happen, not in a million years. Thoughts raced through my mind. What if my mother was right? How would I cope with this news? I hadn't seen them in years. I had even forgotten the faces I once knew because of the long separation. I had to pinch myself to make sure it wasn't a terrible nightmare. Was I awake? A massive earthquake with a magnitude of 7.0

had hit the capital, causing multiple deaths in the blink of an eye. I held a prayer in my heart, pleading with God to please spare my family.

Overcoming heartbreak and finding strength in the face of adversity.

Week after week, I dialed the numbers, desperately seeking confirmation of the unthinkable. "Is it true?" I would ask, my voice trembling with a mix of hope and dread. "Where is Dad?" The answers eluded me, slipping through the cracks of silence. Uncertainty gripped my heart as I yearned for closure.

Then, my uncle's voice broke through the silence on the other end of the line. His words hung heavy in the air, confirming the unimaginable truth—my father was gone. Buried under the rubble, his body lost to the chaos that had consumed our homeland. While we never laid eyes on his physical remains, news reports informed us that his name was among the victims listed under the rubble of collapsed structures. All the bodies and debris were subsequently transported to a mass grave. He was in the midst of teaching a class when the building unexpectedly collapsed. Reports indicated that he was actively and diligently assisting the children to safety, but, unfortunately, he didn't survive the incident.

The weight of this news hit me like a ton of bricks, taking my breath away. All my hopes of reliving precious moments with my father were suddenly crushed, leaving a hole in my heart that could never be filled. The reality of him being gone pierced my soul, casting a dark cloud over my every thought. Regret overwhelmed me as I realized I'd missed the chance to show him how much I loved and appreciated him, lost in the passage of time. Life's fragility became painfully clear, reminding me that tomorrow is never guaranteed.

With my father gone, the glue and pillar of our family, my mother, found herself homeless due to the damage done to our home, and my sister was injured. I desperately wanted to travel to Haiti, but I couldn't find any available flights. I even volunteered with the Red Cross organization to help Haiti and tried to use that as a way to get in contact with my family. As soon as I could, I stood in line at Western Union to send them money and offer support.

During that time, a new phase of tough times started for me. I felt like these challenges were constantly knocking at my door. I was only 21 years old, dealing with grief, money running low, and unable to support myself. I began to wonder if life was being unfair to me. Was this some kind of test from God? The nightmare I was living seemed too strange, too harsh to be real.

Even in the midst of this wreckage, a flash of strength started to grow inside me. Despite my grief, I found the power to face these challenges head-on. The scars of losing my father became a symbol of my strong determination. Even though the pain was overwhelming, I refused to give in to despair. I decided to rise up, changed by the tough times I was going through, and find a way through the darkness.

As I gazed upon the shattered fragments of my family's

life, I became acutely aware of the fragility of existence. Life's unexpected twists and turns taught me the profound importance of cherishing those we hold dear. No longer would I withhold my feelings or leave my thoughts left unspoken. I vowed to seize every opportunity to express love, gratitude, and appreciation, for the tomorrow we yearn for may never come.

Though the loss of my father, the homelessness of my mother, and my sister's severe injuries cast a long shadow over me, I refused to succumb to bitterness. Instead, I stood tall in my role as a beacon of hope, a guiding light in chaos. Adversity had become my constant companion, but it would not define me. I would weave a new narrative, one of resilience, compassion, and unwavering determination.

Amidst this nightmare, I clung to the belief that there was a purpose to my journey. Though the answers eluded me, I summoned the strength to endure. The road ahead was tough, but I wouldn't be defeated. As I rose from the ashes of my old life, I was transformed. The trials left scars but also ignited a fire within me. I committed to turning my pain into purpose, my grief into a force for change. This is my journey, a testament to the human spirit's resilience. I refused to be defined by victimhood and embraced challenges, knowing they would shape me into a stronger, more compassionate version of myself.

People often ask if I've come to terms with my father's death. The truth is, I never fully have. The pain remains, and I still yearn for moments with him. But I've found solace in honoring his memory by bringing hope and positive change to others. I can only imagine that if my father were alive, he'd want me to strive for greatness and make a difference. He was my role model, and his belief in me still resonates within my soul.

Two years passed after the earthquake before I could visit Haiti. Seeing my childhood home in ruins was heartwrenching. I returned for my sister's wedding, representing my dad by walking my sister to the altar. The void left by his absence was palpable. The same happened when my wedding day arrived, Dad's absence was deeply felt. Through loss and sorrow, we found optimism. We cherished the time spent with our loved ones, understanding the preciousness of each day.

CHAPTER 5

Hitting Rock Bottom

How I Pulled Through My Darkest Moments

After the untimely passing of my father, life in the United States grew increasingly burdensome. The weight of grief and financial hardship bore down on me, enveloping my days in deep sorrow. As I continued my journey towards personal growth and the pursuit of better income, I began to explore new opportunities. Tired of my job at the supermarket, I sought a more fulfilling and rewarding career. Working as a cashier was a good experience, but I felt stuck because there were no opportunities for growth.

One of my co-workers from the supermarket had moved on to work at Home Depot. He mentioned the significantly higher pay and the potential for career advancement in his new role. This information ignited a dream within me, and I set my sights on working at Home Depot. I went home the same night and applied for a sales associate position. Unfortunately, after 2 months I still hadn't received an email for an interview.

Nonetheless, I didn't allow this setback to discourage me. A few months later, I made the decision to reapply for a position at Home Depot. That time, I received a call from talent acquisition for an interview, I was nervous and excited, uncertain about how everything would unfold. But I knew it was for the best.

That evening, I got ready, my hands trembling with excitement for what lay ahead. The next morning, I woke up early, ready to begin something that would challenge my determination. I took the bus to Coney Island Station, hopped on the N train, transferred to the R train, and at last arrived at the Prospect Avenue stop in Brooklyn. From there, I walked all the way to the store.

Finally, I arrived in front of a Huge Home Depot sign. Standing in front of the building, I grappled with self-doubt and anxiety. Questions raced through my mind. Was I making a fool out of myself? How would I fully understand the questions given my language barrier? I had been down this road before, and even though my ability to converse had improved, I was still far from being an expert.

As the hour of the interview approached, I realized there was no turning back. I summoned the courage to face my fears. I approached the customer service desk and asked for directions to the manager's office.

"Are you Kevin?" asked the service desk associate, my name was listed as a scheduled interview candidate, so they kindly guided me through the back of the store.

Walking through a long aisle, I passed various departments – electrical, appliance showroom, paint desk, flooring, and receiving. Finally, I arrived at my destination, an office located in the far corner of the building.

"Have a seat," said the associate who escorted me to the back office. I waited anxiously, aware there had been a few candidates before me. My heart pounded, and doubts crept in. *What if the position had already been filled? What if I don't get hired?*

An older gentlemen walked towards me asking, "Are you Kevin?" *Yes*, I answered in my head while nodding, my heart leapt into my throat. "Follow me," he urged as I followed him into the office. "Have a seat; don't be nervous!" he shouted.

He introduced himself and started with a simple statement, "Tell me a little bit about yourself." I almost froze and asked him to repeat himself. While responding in my head, I tried to figure out how my words would come across. I gave it my best shot. Question after question, I was surviving.

The last question came posed as a scenario. He asked me about assembling a trimmer for a display, a task assigned to me by a manager, "How would you handle this task?" To this day, I'm not sure how I answered that question or if he even understood my response. I gathered all the English words I could find and threw them at him with gesture, English words mixed with French and Creole. I was determined and hungry for a new work environment. I had come too far to lose now.

He looked down at the paperwork and said, "Well, Kevin, if you have the will to do it…you can do it." Relief dropped over me before he added, "I want to offer you the job."

August 2010, I got hired as a Merchandising Execution Team associate (MET). In this role, I was responsible for creating displays, performing maintenance in store bays, and completing various projects. It marked a significant shift from my previous job as a cashier. I had faith that it was the right step for my life.

The potential for accomplishment in life knows no bounds. No matter the obstacles that stand in your path, it is crucial to summon the strength to fight back. If language poses a challenge, seek ways to conquer it. Whatever the hurdle may be, refuse to surrender and instead find a way to achieve success. Remember, giving up is not an option. With determination and perseverance, the seemingly impossible can become possible.

I was genuinely excited about this new opportunity. However, night after night, tears streamed down my face as I grappled with overwhelming emotions, still mourning the loss of my dad. During this turbulent period, both my cousin and I found ourselves teetering on the brink of homelessness, unsure of where to turn next.

The building management began conducting inspections, and we weren't registered as residents with the housing department. The situation became untenable, and we were forced to leave the Coney Island apartment we had called home. The pastor who had sheltered us could no longer provide assistance. This left my cousin and me with no other option but to begin the daunting task of finding somewhere else to live.

Amidst the darkness, a glimmer of hope emerged. I persisted, making numerous phone calls and conducting thorough searches. Eventually, I found a room for rent that suited my needs. My determination extended to helping my cousin, and I continued my efforts until I secured a separate room for him as well.

The challenge we faced was the monthly rent of $500, which nearly consumed my entire monthly paycheck. It was a significant financial burden, but we had no other choice; we had to leave the building. So, I made the best of our circumstances by surviving on a meager diet of bread, peanut butter, and juice, before and after work. Despite the limited provisions, I pressed forward.

Unfortunately, my financial situation deteriorated to the

point where affording the rented room was no longer feasible. This dire circumstance forced me to seek refuge in a basement, a dim and dusty space that offered little comfort. After moving to this basement, where I had secured a room for rent, I discovered an extra room available.

Recognizing the financial hardships, we both faced, I saw an opportunity to invite my cousin to join me in this new living arrangement. Despite the limited resources, I selflessly sacrificed the bed and chose to sleep on cardboard, ensuring my cousin had a more comfortable place to rest. Our shared commitment to supporting each other through challenges strengthened our bond and determination to overcome adversity.

The reality of my situation hit me with an unrelenting force, plunging me into the darkest chapter of my life. One night, as I lay on the basement floor, a roach crawled onto my face, abruptly waking me from my sleep. Startled, I quickly got up to kill it. The incident left me unable to find peace or sleep for the rest of the night. My mind was consumed with troubling thoughts, and the discomfort lingered, reminding me of the challenges I faced daily. I found myself in a state of self-neglect, burdened by a poor attitude and a negative mindset, convinced that greatness would forever elude me. Even my appearance seemed to reflect my pessimistic thoughts.

In the depths of that basement, I confronted a crushing sense of hopelessness. The weight of my grief combined with the bleakness of my living conditions pushed me to the brink of despair. Thoughts of suicide permeated my mind, as I felt utterly trapped and without any possibility of redemption. The loneliness and helplessness I experienced were overwhelming, casting a shadow of shame upon my existence.

I can confidently say living in the basement marked the lowest point in my life. As I stared at those grim walls, I couldn't help but reflect on the stark contrast between the first part of my life and my current situation. It led me to question how I had arrived at this point. With each passing year, I found myself sinking into debt, barely making ends meet with each paycheck. I spent my days and nights contemplating how to rebuild my life. I was navigating uncharted waters, trying to figure out life entirely on my own. It was during this time that I realized the unpredictability of life. We never truly know where this journey will take us, and we must always be prepared for the unexpected.

The basement owner was quite strict about rent payments, and he made it clear that he expected his money on time every month. Consequently, I made it a priority to set aside the basement rent before allocating any funds for myself. The monthly rent for the basement was $900, which my cousin and I split evenly.

The living conditions in the basement were far from ideal. It had a small stove and fridge, and an old-fashioned blue tub. Every morning, we would wake up to find it infested with water bugs. Moreover, the basement lacked a proper heating system, so we had to rely on the warmth from the boiler pipe that ran from the main floor to provide some heat. We tried to discreetly introduce personal heaters, but the homeowner forbade us from doing so, citing concerns about a significant increase in his electricity bill. Despite this, we went ahead with the heaters to make the living conditions more bearable.

Finding the courage to face challenges head-on.

While I was living in the basement and working at Home Depot, I decided to take advantage of the company's benefits, which included tuition reimbursement. My goal was to re-enroll in college and further my education. However, to accommodate my school schedule, I needed to switch departments as the MET department's schedule was from Monday through Friday. I put in a request to transfer to a store associate role, which was granted along with my scheduling request for school.

Initially, I was determined to continue my education, believing it would lead to better job opportunities in the future. However, after completing the first semester, I found myself postponing the process due to a lack of funds. My focus shifted towards work and making more money, making it my top priority at the time.

One day, while completing a task in the flooring department, a young supervisor in charge of receiving approached me with a straightforward question: "Would you like to work in my department?" I enthusiastically said yes because it was a chance to shift from merchandising to an operational department. I saw it as an opportunity to expand my knowledge and advance within the company.

The following week, the store manager called me into their office and proposed a department switch. Without hesitation I agreed, again, grateful for the chance to learn new skills and be a part of the operational side of the company. The prospect of growth and development brought me a sense of happiness and anticipation.

As I pressed on, giving my best in the department and maintaining a positive attitude, my manager began to recognize something special in me. However, behind the scenes, I was still grappling with the difficult circumstances of my home life—sleeping on a humble piece of cardboard in a basement. I was determined to keep this reality hidden from others, unwilling to let anyone know the extent of my struggle.

Due to my financial difficulties, I couldn't afford necessities like food and clothing. I was torn between the prospect of joining the army and the much more dire thought of ending my life because of shame, loneliness, mounting debt, and a feeling of helplessness. My spirit was at its lowest point, and I found myself completely destitute.

With no money left to my name, I had made a crucial investment by spending my last remaining dollar on a monthly metro card to be able to ride the public transit system. This decision was necessary to ensure my punctuality and dedication in making it to work every day.

My supervisor back then was a genuinely kind person who had faith in me. He often gave me extra tasks because he knew I'd always put in 100% effort to complete them excellently. I admired his enthusiasm, especially considering he was a young leader, close to my age, already in a supervisory role. Gradually, my manager recognized my potential and took it upon himself to mentor me further because I was always eager to learn and take on new challenges.

At one point, when the department needed to cut hours and transfer employees to other departments, my manager chose to keep me in receiving. I was the only one who stayed, and this strengthened our professional relationship. We talked about a wide range of topics, and our bond grew stronger over time.

One day, we started talking about life's struggles. In that moment, I mustered the courage to share my story with him. I revealed that for months, I had been sleeping in a basement on a humble piece of cardboard. I confided that I had contemplated quitting and searching for another job, as I desperately needed more money. My words hung in the air, showing the depth of my struggle and vulnerability.

In an unexpected turn of events, my manager told me to take a 15-minute break. He swiftly left, jumping into his car and driving away. As I returned to work after my break, diligently completing my tasks, my manager reappeared, holding an envelope. Intrigued, I asked him what it was. Instead of answering, he simply instructed me to open it.

I tore open the envelope, discovering $600. Stunned, I expressed my intent to repay him. However, he kindly replied that he didn't expect the money back. His true intention was to inspire and motivate me. He requested one promise: that I would not quit because there was immense potential within me. He assured me that I had yet to fully realize my capabilities, and he envisioned a bright future for me with the company. In fact, he went so far as to suggest that one day, I might even become his boss.

It wasn't solely about the money, although I used it wisely. I bought an air mattress, upgrading from the cardboard on which I had been sleeping on for months. After a little while, each morning I would find myself on the floor, diligently patching up the air mattress to make it last. I also utilized the remaining funds to take care of pressing bills. The true significance of this act of kindness lay in the hope and belief my supervisor instilled in me.

For the first time, someone saw my potential and believed in me. Despite the troubles I had faced and the doubts that plagued me, he recognized the greatness hidden within me. This newfound belief sparked a fire within my soul, igniting a sense of purpose and possibility. I was able to see a glimpse of the extraordinary potential that had been there all along, waiting to be unleashed.

This experience changed the course of my life. It only takes one person to believe in you, to light the fire within and set you on a path of greatness. Inspired by my manager's solid support, I began to reshape my attitude and outlook. Recognizing that success begins with self-confidence and a positive mindset, I decided to take a proactive step towards achieving my goals. I saved some money from each paycheck and made my way to the mall at the end of each month, fully aware that my appearance could influence how I felt and how others perceived me. With a renewed sense of purpose and determination, I invested in new clothes that symbolized my commitment to personal growth and success.

I was incredibly fortunate to have a supervisor who was not only invested in my professional growth but also deeply cared about my overall well-being. His commitment to my success went above and beyond the call of duty, leaving a lasting impact on my life.

Every morning, he would personally pick me up, understanding the financial constraints I faced, along with the challenges of commuting. This small gesture of kindness and support made a significant difference in my daily life, relieving me of the additional financial burden and ensuring I could focus on my work without worries.

During our shared lunches, we would not only discuss work-related matters but also engage in conversations that fostered personal growth. He became not just a supervisor but a mentor, offering guidance, wisdom, and valuable insights that helped shape my professional journey. At the end of each workday, he made it a point to ensure my safe travel home, he inspired me, he became my big brother. I used to ask him all the time, "When will I be like you?"

He'd respond, "Trust the process and one day your day will come."

However, it wasn't only he who extended such support.

Other supervisors at the company also embraced me as part of the Home Depot family. They, too, were willing to lend a helping hand, offering me rides home when my supervisor was off or on vacation, and treating me with warmth and respect. This culture of support and camaraderie within the company created an environment where I felt valued and included. I have never worked for such a company before.

The remarkable culture at Home Depot positively altered my perception of work. It was no longer just a place to earn a paycheck, but a community of individuals who genuinely cared about each other's success and well-being.

Their support allowed me to thrive in my role. Their acts of kindness, guidance, and inclusion instilled in me a sense of belonging and motivated me to push myself further. They became my daily inspiration. Witnessing their growth and success within the company ignited a fire within me, motivating me to work even harder and strive for my own professional advancement. Their journeys served as a testament to the growth potential awaiting within the organization, and I was determined to seize every opportunity that came my way.

CHAPTER 6

A Journey of Self-Discovery and Success

How a Home Depot Employee's Determination and Inspiration Transformed a So Called "Dead-End Job" into a Life-Changing Career

One night, as I walked into the store to work overnight, helping the night manager unload trucks to ensure receiving was neat and organized, I had the life-changing opportunity to listen to a motivational speaker named Eric "ET" Thomas. His speech was truly one of the greatest I had ever heard, and its impact on my life was profound. One of the key messages that resonated with me was his statement, "When you want to succeed as bad as you want to breathe, then you will be successful." During his captivating speech, Eric Thomas shared a thought-provoking analogy about a young man seeking guidance from a guru. The story goes as follows:

The young man, filled with ambition and a burning desire for success, approached the wise guru seeking the secret to achieving his dreams. Eagerly, he asked the guru, "How can I become successful?"

In response, the guru led the young man towards a nearby river. As they stood by the water's edge, the guru suddenly pushed the young man's head underwater, holding it there. The young man struggled desperately, gasping for air, but the guru continued to keep his head submerged.

After what felt like an eternity, the guru finally released the young man and allowed him to breathe again. The young man, confused and frustrated, asked the guru, "Why did you do that? What does it have to do with success?"

The guru calmly replied, "When you were underwater, what did you want more than anything else?"

Struggling to catch his breath, the young man exclaimed, "Air! I wanted to breathe!"

The guru smiled and said, "Exactly. When you want success as much as you wanted to breathe, then you will find it. Success demands that level of hunger, that unwavering commitment and determination."

Through this analogy, Eric Thomas emphasizes the importance of having an intense and relentless desire for success. Just as we instinctively prioritize breathing to sustain our lives, he suggests success requires the same level of urgency and dedication.

This became my motto for that year. I wanted to make a difference, I wanted to be successful. My work ethic also inspired my supervisor, who 6 months later earned a well-deserved promotion. This created a vacancy in his previous position. I saw it as the perfect chance to step up and fill the role. I was ready and eager to take on the added responsibilities and challenges that came with the position. I was hungry and determined; I had already claimed that position. So, I applied to be interviewed.

Although confident, I was also nervous after applying for an overnight supervisor position earlier that year and did not get selected. A few days later, I had the opportunity to be interviewed, but this time I had all the experience needed already working in the department.

The interview process went smoothly. I was able to navigate the questions easily and provide answers based on my receiving experience, I had seen it all.

The following week, the store manager called me into the office for a second interview and 3 days later, I was offered the position.

My first-ever promotion. I felt a mixture of excitement and determination. This promotion marked a significant milestone in my career, as it not only recognized my hard work and dedication but also presented a considerable financial breakthrough.

The increase in income from my new role allowed me to save money and purchase a used car, which was a game-changer. It made my daily commute to work much easier and more convenient. No longer reliant on public transportation or the generosity of others, I gained a newfound sense of independence and freedom. While it wasn't the greatest car in the world, it got me from point A to point B.

My first promotion was quite challenging. As a supervisor, I needed to learn how to lead a team while staying true to myself. Some people believe that when they move up in their career, they have to change who they are. I wanted to prove that being authentic is just as important as the title I held. I remained the same Kevin; but, I had to find ways to help my team excel in receiving. The plan was to create multiple Kevins.

It wasn't an easy journey. I went through two different teams before I found the right formula. The turning point was when I decided to be involved in the hiring process. I wanted to inspire candidates from the very beginning, even before they joined my department. It paid off when I discovered two exceptional team members. I was ready to teach, train, and lead them to unlock their full potential.

On the other hand, despite the promotion and the increased income that allowed me to afford a car, I still lived in a basement. However, my determination remained strong. I had a clear goal: motivating others by sharing my life story and humble beginnings. I went from being a janitor not even qualified to work as a cashier at McDonald's to now leading a team for an amazing company. I had a newfound purpose, and I wanted to convey the message that if it could happen for me, it could happen for anyone with belief and hard work.

I began speaking to every person who entered the receiving area, delivering an inspirational message. They didn't have much of a choice whether or not to listen since they had to come to receiving to crush their boxes or dispose of their trash. This became my opportunity to practice crafting and delivering my message to them.

Every morning, we had a meeting called the "pep rally," and it was my chance to motivate others with morning quotes and positivity to start the day. I made it a point to do this every day I worked.

Then, one day, our store manager asked all the department supervisors to introduce themselves to the new hires during their orientation. As each supervisor said their name and the department they managed, I took a different approach. I began my speech by sharing my humble beginnings and how far I had come, all while delivering motivational quotes. I explained to the new employees that their journey with the company could be a life-changing experience, depending on what they made of it.

The impact was profound. Everyone was taken aback, unaware that I had been preparing for this day for months by speaking to each associate who entered my receiving department. Weeks later, some of those new hires approached me to express how my speech had inspired them to keep pushing forward.

One day, while in the receiving department, feeling a bit down, an idea came to me. I decided to record a video to post on Twitter. The message was clear: never give up, keep pushing, and keep moving forward, no matter the circumstances, because we worked for a great company. I added the hashtag #InspirationalFridays, as I recorded it on a Friday.

Little did I know this video would resonate, not only with my colleagues at the company, but also with a much larger audience on social media. This video had a ripple effect and marked the beginning of my incredible journey as a motivator.

Not long after, a significant shift happened in my mindset. Complaints and disappointments were replaced with a new motto: "Obstacles inspire growth." This fresh perspective motivated me to actively engage in every store and departmental project, whether it was a pilot program or a new process. My aim was to play a crucial role in solving problems.

I came to realize a fundamental truth: success is shaped by the ability to confront challenges head-on.

This transformation, however, came with its own set of challenges. It required a three-year commitment to elevate the receiving department to the pinnacle of excellence. During this time, I was also grooming a successor, knowing that my time in this position was limited.

With confidence, I adopted a unique ritual: I greeted every associate who entered my department with a handshake and these words, "Remember me, my name is Kevin Marius, and soon I'll be leaving the store as an assistant store manager." Skepticism hung in the air because the store hadn't witnessed a promotion since my last supervisor became a salary leader. Nevertheless, I stood tall and remained focused. My goal was no longer just about me; it was about leaving a legacy.

In retrospect, my rise from novice to influencer demonstrates that leadership is more than a title; it is a dynamic force that arises from inside. My story shows how even humble beginnings can generate significant transformation, and every obstacle is a steppingstone on the path to success.

I vividly recall how the assistant managers used to share their amazing experiences in Atlanta with me. The company would send all newly promoted salary leaders to Atlanta for a week of training, and it was described as nothing short of incredible. I used these stories as a source of motivation to keep pushing myself forward. However, things took a turn when my store manager left, and a new manager took over. She was new to the role, and I felt my plans were disrupted with the change. I became frustrated and contemplated transferring to another store.

During this period of uncertainty, the new manager had

a conversation with me that made me pause and reflect. I started questioning myself: *Why was I running away?* Remember, obstacles inspire growth. I felt the need to stay and continue working on myself, inspiring others in the store and on Twitter, and developing my associates. That year, we achieved the best numbers for inventory ever recorded. This was a testament to my hard work in an operational department.

I devised new plans to reduce shrink, focusing on educating all associates and leaders, and reinforcing receiving processes and paperwork. Receiving had a significant impact, and we established a new receiving standard.

During that same year, I achieved the position of high-performance supervisor. I diligently completed all the required training and was chosen to take the retail management assessment test (RMA), a crucial step towards becoming an assistant store manager. I successfully passed the RMA test, leading to the next phase, which involved two interview processes.

A week after receiving the news of my test success, I was

scheduled for the interview processes. On the day of the interviews, I waited in the room with a mix of anticipation and uncertainty. When it was my turn, I walked into the interview room knowing I had given my best. A week later, I successfully completed both the FIT and PIT interviews.

As I awaited a response, my heart raced with anticipation, unsure whether I had left a positive impression or needed constructive feedback. However, there was no time to dwell on it as we had to prepare for a quarterly district walk.

On the day of the walk, while touring my department, my manager engaged in a series of probing questions that both intrigued me and left me uncertain about the purpose. Suddenly, my District Manager reached for the phone, dialing a number that would unexpectedly alter my path. He explained that the voice on the other end belonged to a representative from the corporate headquarters in Atlanta, and there was a need for a discussion regarding paperwork compliance.

As I took the phone, a wave of realization swept over me – it was the store manager, the very individual who had previously interviewed me, now on the line. In the background, joyful sounds erupted, voices joining in a harmonic chorus to convey the uplifting news: "Congratulations, Kevin! You've been promoted!" The enormity of the occasion, the culmination of years of hard work and sacrifice, overwhelmed me. Flooded with an array of emotions, I found myself moved to tears – tears that flowed freely, akin to a newborn's cry.

In that emotional moment, a rush of delight, gratitude, and humility came over me, coupled with a profound sense of accomplishment. I had crossed the barrier of dreams, moving into the reality that I had previously desired. The tears that fell were more than just an expression of personal success; they reflected the recognition of a never-ending journey, the embodiment of countless hours invested, and embracing a future yet to be reached.

In the midst of my weeping, I came to a fork in the road between my past and my future. It was a moment that encompassed the essence of transformation, a snapshot in time when dreams met reality and the seeds of determination grew. Through my tears, I saw a new chapter unfolding, one full of opportunity, challenges, and the possibility of progress. As congratulatory sentiments echoed around me, I realized that this was more than just a promotion; it was the culmination of resilience, a testament to the pursuit of excellence, and a celebration of the road that had led me to this incredible juncture.

A few months after I completed my training as an assistant store manager, my district manager came to meet with me. During our conversation in his office, his words felt like precious gems, etching a lasting impression on my heart and pointing the way forward. He emphasized, "With each promotion, it's like hitting a reset button; you no longer hold all the answers. It's an opportunity to refine your skills." This counsel remained with me as a steady guide, offering valuable insights and direction.

Let me share a story with you.

This story teaches us a valuable lesson about the importance of self-care, continuous improvement, and not just working hard, but working smart. Here's the revised version of the story:

Once upon a time in a tranquil village, a strong woodcutter sought employment with a timber merchant. He was hired promptly, attracted by the good pay and favorable working conditions. Eager to excel, the woodcutter was determined to give his best.

His new boss handed him an axe and indicated the area where he was to work.

On the first day, the woodcutter managed to bring down an impressive 18 trees.

"Congratulations!" the boss exclaimed. "Keep up the excellent work!"

Motivated by his boss' praise, the woodcutter pushed himself harder the next day. However, he could only fell 15 trees. Despite his best efforts, the following day yielded even fewer trees—only 10.

Doubt began to creep into the woodcutter's mind. *Am I losing my strength?* he wondered. Distressed by his declining performance, he approached the boss and confessed his bewilderment.

The boss calmly inquired, "When was the last time you sharpened your axe?"

"Sharpened my axe?" the woodcutter replied, bewildered. "I've been too busy cutting trees to find the time for that."

The boss smiled kindly and said, "My friend, sharpening your axe is not a waste of time but an investment in your efficiency. With a sharp axe, you can accomplish more in less time."

Realizing the wisdom of his boss' words, the woodcutter took the time to sharpen his axe. When he returned to the forest, he was amazed at how easily the blade sliced through the trees. He started bringing down trees faster and more effortlessly than before.

From that day forward, he made it a point to regularly sharpen his axe, ensuring his efforts were always as effective as possible.

Using that story, the district manager imparted a profound truth: The story of the woodcutter emphasizes the importance of self-care, continuous improvement, and working smart rather than just hard.

This encounter with my district manager became a pivotal moment, altering the course of my life's narrative. His counsel emerged as a cornerstone of my success, a principle carried with me through every twist and turn, every accomplishment and setback.

My greatest memory during this time was when the HR Manager handed me the paperwork to negotiate my new salary, it was double what I was making. I froze, my hand shaking, all of a sudden I forgot how to sign. "This is a life-changing experience," said my District Manager. Indeed, it was. Not only the salary but I was also offered company shares and a bonus. This is the same place people used to tell me to quit because it was labeled a 'dead-end job' that somehow had changed my life. Being part of the Home Depot was one of the greatest decisions I have ever made.

My manager at that time played a crucial role in my promotion and continued to support me as a mentor. We have maintained a strong connection that continues to this day. I am grateful for her guidance and encouragement throughout my journey. She never stopped believing in me. One of her favorite quotes is by Napoleon Hill, "Whatever the mind can conceive and believe, it can achieve." All this started with a thought that others before me have done it, which meant it was possible for me. But, I had to change my mindset and start to believe in myself. Each day, I reminded myself of the goal and created a game plan around it, until it became a reality.

The next step was to figure out how to replicate it. To prove to others that it is possible. The blueprint was created by the leaders before me, it was not just a gamble, it was a formula; applied the right way, promotion would come.

The promotion aligned perfectly with my upcoming

wedding, marking a period of celebration and fulfillment in our lives. It provided us with greater confidence and security for planning our future together. With the increased income, I was able to comfortably afford a two-bedroom apartment saying goodbye to the basement and embraced a more comfortable, spacious living arrangement.

CHAPTER 7

From Challenges to Triumph

"From Comfort Zones to Career Milestones: A Journey of Resilience and Growth"

Embarking on a new challenge, promoted to a high-volume store in Brooklyn while simultaneously navigating life's complexities as a newlywed. This shift was a departure from my usual routine. In the dynamic store environment, I faced the task of leading a large portion of the business, responsible for multiple departments such as Building Materials, Lumber and Millwork specialty department, dealing with Pro Contractors. It was no longer solely about completing tasks but mastering the art of influential leadership. Becoming a servant leader and influencer at a high level.

Starting as a young leader, having managing supervisors who were often much older than me posed a distinct challenge. Their initial mindset was likely questioning the authority of this young leader telling them what to do. While I might have been young in age, significant experience brought me to this point. I possessed the determination and drive that many leaders often lack.

Fortunately, I had exceptional peers who provided invaluable mentorship. At Home Depot, it's like a big family, and other leaders are always willing to offer advice and guide you step-by-step. In addition, the company provides leadership training at its Atlanta headquarters, which added significant value to my preparation for the new responsibilities ahead. The training was truly life-changing and equipped me with the skills needed to lead effectively. Before my promotion to Assistant Store Manager, I used to hear managers talk about this training.

I used to wonder if the amazing training at the company's Atlanta headquarters would ever be possible for me. I couldn't believe it when my turn finally came, and I found myself on a plane, feeling like I was dreaming. "Am I really going to Atlanta?" I asked myself in disbelief.

I remember a message from one of our facilitators during the training: "This training is just the base, and it will be up to you to apply it and make a difference in your stores and the people you'll be leading. Most importantly, years from now, some of you will be promoted, some might give up, and some will become legendary." This message changed my mindset. It was a journey to get there, but I envisioned myself changing others' lives and inspiring people on a different level. I aimed to create my brand within the company. However, reality hits you once you board the plane and face the real challenges on a day-to-day basis. It's not easy to stay motivated. It takes courage to practice self-motivation. Countless times, I wanted to give up and question if this was right for me. Challenges can push you to doubt your drive, but you have to find focus deep inside to remember the "why." You need to recall what got you here in the first place and where you're headed.

For me, I started at the bottom, living in a basement, financially unstable. I went from working as a janitor at McDonald's to becoming a cashier at a supermarket, and eventually, I became a regular associate and then an assistant store manager. I reminded myself that I must keep pushing and be a beacon of hope for other associates like me, showing them that it's possible. I believed in the company culture that said I could climb the ladder and even become a CEO.

I saw a poster in the breakroom displaying all the leaders who started from the bottom and had reached executive leadership positions. I envisioned myself on that poster, inspiring someone else. Eventually, Years later, I made it onto a similar poster that was displayed in every store. The company produced a documentary called "Behind the Apron" and an Orange magazine article, highlighting my career path. I received numerous emails from others saying my story inspired them to keep pushing. There's nothing greater in life than when you start dreaming and believing in yourself. God created you to be great, so there is greatness within you. The best part was that there was already a blueprint, and all I had to do was follow it and continue to pay it forward.

As time passed, I delved deeper into understanding the intricate dynamics of the store, it wasn't easy. It was the second largest volume store in the New York Metro Region. I recognized that adapting my leadership style to genuinely inspire my team was the key to success. I needed to find a way to influence both my team and the entire store. My approach was to think, "In my previous role, I could impact and influence my department and a few others. How can I replicate that success and now inspire supervisors and the entire store?"

I came to the realization that I needed to make a change and embrace a servant leadership approach. I understood that to lead effectively, I must first serve and set an example for my team. While others advised Assistant Store Managers (ASMs) to stop certain tasks when they assumed their roles, I chose to demonstrate to my team that I wouldn't ask them to do anything I wouldn't do myself. If there was a pallet to be dropped for a customer, I did it as an ASM. I assisted my supervisors in departmental walks, assisting with the pack out process, and even in merchandise ordering. I made sure to teach them the importance of maintaining in-stock levels and I delved into the details of merchandising, like understanding ASW (Average Sales per Week) and analyzing sales and comparisons to boost average sales and gross margins. I began teaching my team the reasoning behind our methods.

Not only did the supervisors benefit from this approach, but the associates as well. We would walk through an area once, and within weeks, we noticed a significant difference. It was no longer just about packing out; they started to take ownership of the business. Once I revealed my deep passion and invited them on a journey, piece-by-piece, sharing my own story of how far I had come, I realized the incredible power I possessed to motivate and inspire others. I began to make a significant impact on their lives, and in return, they started to have faith in me because I led by example.

To this day, they still reach out to express their gratitude for the positive influence I had on them. I taught them that in order to lead, we must first care. I made it a point to know everything about their personal lives, including their kids. Some days, I even went the extra mile by purchasing movie tickets for the associates and their families. I'd tell them, "I know you have the weekend off, take your family to the movies on me." It was my way of showing appreciation for all the hard work they put in. They were willing to move mountains for me because they knew I cared about them.

As leaders, we need to shift our focus away from just metrics and numbers and concentrate on the people because, without them, there are no Key Performance Indicators (KPIs). Instead, we should aim to use KPI as "Keep People

Inspired." By doing so, you'll achieve better results. I've applied this approach in all of my leadership roles, both in the store and the supply chain.

Many people often ask me how I climbed the career ladder as quickly as I did, and the simple answer is that I was willing to do what others wouldn't. I sought opportunities that others might have overlooked. I volunteered for roles that were initially less appealing to my peers. I stepped into positions like inventory captain, which was challenging. Spending late nights prepping for weeks, I asked myself why had I agreed to complete this additional task. A continual path of growth meant I had to be uncomfortable to learn from new experiences. The best way to grow is to face adversity, and the best way to get to the next level is to solve a problem.

Growth often occurs outside our comfort zones. When we remain in a state of comfort, we tend to stick to familiar routines and habits, which can limit our personal and professional development. It's when we challenge ourselves, embrace new experiences, and step into the unknown that we truly expand our horizons. I excelled in my career and achieved my current position by being willing to volunteer for various tasks and never saying 'no' to a learning opportunity when one presented itself. It's the key to my success, and I'm grateful for it.

Stepping out of our comfort zones can be uncomfortable and even intimidating, but it's in these moments of discomfort that we learn, adapt, and grow. We acquire new skills, gain fresh perspectives, and discover strengths we never knew we had. It's the path to self-improvement and the key to unlocking our full potential.

So, remember, while comfort provides a sense of security, it's in discomfort that we find seeds of growth. Embrace challenges, take risks, and be open to change, for it is in these moments you'll discover your true potential and achieve remarkable personal and professional growth.

As I reflect on experiences such as changing the standard of service, spearheading developmental changes, and raising new leaders, I offer the following advice. In the journey toward personal growth and the pursuit of greatness, one pivotal lesson stands out: the power of shifting perspective from complaining to problem-solving. Complaining about life's challenges may provide momentary relief, but it seldom leads to meaningful change or progress. In contrast, problem-solvers are the architects of their destiny. They embrace challenges as steppingstones to success, channeling their energy into finding solutions rather than dwelling on problems. This shift in mindset is the beacon that illuminates the path to personal growth and opens doors to a future where success knows no bounds. If you aspire to excel in life, dare to be a problem-solver, for therein lies the key to unlocking your full potential and achieving the greatness that resides within you.

Every task assigned to me by my store manager was seen as an opportunity to hone my skills. My philosophy has always been to give 100% in everything I do. When I was a janitor at McDonald's, I took pride in being the best. I cleaned the windows and toilets better than anyone else. I was the one who meticulously mopped the floor, and prepared the soda and ketchup. When I later worked at the supermarket, I knew all the product codes better than anyone. In fact, even now, I go to the supermarket and often have to remind cashiers of the vegetable codes when they forget. This shows my determination to excel in what I do.

The same mentality carried over when I joined Home Depot. I wanted to be the best flooring associate and the best receiving associate. I eagerly learned what others were afraid to tackle and became an expert in those areas. When my manager asked for an assistant manager to handle overnight shifts, I excelled on every weekend, ensuring that the manager responsible for freight had a successful start to the new week without any backlogs. My manager was astonished by my reliability and decided to promote me to Operations Manager.

Have you ever heard the quote, "Be so good that they can't ignore you"? That was my guiding principle. I took on the role with a clear game plan to make a difference in operations. I implemented effective structures to set operations up for success, improved customer service, and reduced operational shrink throughout the entire store. It was a supportive role where I had to learn how to motivate my peers and gain their buy-in. I realized that you're only as strong as your team. Even if you're not the coach, you have to figure out how to motivate while being on the court. You must believe that when you're being guarded, you should pass the ball to the open shooter and trust their ability to make the shot. If they miss, you have to be ready to play defense and grab the rebound for another opportunity. This experience significantly enhanced my leadership skills.

As an Operations Manager, I recognized the importance of networking. During various operational walks, I had the opportunity to meet a Talent Acquisition Manager. Little did I know, he was related to one of my associates in my department. I used to celebrate his birthday by giving him a Starbucks gift card, as he was a fan of their coffee. Unbeknownst to me, his brother was the Talent Acquisition Manager. We had the chance to meet during a store visit, and we formed a strong bond. He saw potential in me, and we've maintained a connection ever since.

This experience taught me a valuable lesson: every meeting is essentially like a job interview, and everyone you meet represents an opportunity. It's crucial never to underestimate the value of meeting exceptional individuals. Keep their contact information and nurture these connections, as they may be the ones who open doors to numerous opportunities in the future.

A year later, I received a life-changing call from the Talent Acquisition Manager I'd met earlier. He presented me with an opportunity to join the company's new project, the Market Delivery Operation Cross Dock. This role was offered to me because months prior I had expressed my interest in the supply chain industry, and the Talent Acquisition Manager believed I was the perfect fit for the project. His guidance and encouragement to pursue this position turned out to be a pivotal decision that marked my transition to the supply chain field and changed the course of my career.

I had the privilege of interviewing with a Supply Chain Manager who recognized my immense potential right away. Our connection was immediate, and he expressed his belief that I would be a perfect fit for the team he was building. A few weeks later, I received the exciting news that I was hired as an Area Supervisor in the Elizabeth,

New Jersey Market Delivery Operations. I was thrilled to receive the call, and I showed the news to my wife. We prayed together before signing the offer letter, grateful for this new opportunity.

This new role came with a significant challenge – we had a tight deadline to fully staff the building, and we had to hit the ground running. Despite the difficulties, we successfully met our staffing goals ahead of schedule. With the team in place, it was time to prepare the building for its grand opening.

Following a successful go-live, I had another chance to travel to Atlanta for training. When I returned to New Jersey, I was honored to receive the Value-Based Leader Award, which was voted on by my peers during the training. It was a meaningful experience to share my journey with them. During this time, I realized that my ability to motivate was taking me down a different path. I became an inspiration not only for new leaders but also for those in higher roles. It was a reminder never to limit who you can inspire.

In 2020, my wife and I made the decision to relocate to New Jersey, not only because it was closer to work but also because we wanted to pursue our dream of buying a home. Since we began our journey as a married couple, we faced numerous obstacles in New York, including a lender who deemed it impossible for us to secure a loan. We were devastated, but from that point forward, I made a promise to myself that I would do whatever it took to overcome that obstacle, and we would never hear another "no."

Have you ever been told "no" and refused to accept it as the final answer? I learned years ago that when someone tells you "no," you should ask them for the reasons behind it and then begin working on those tips to turn it into a "yes."

During this time, I played a pivotal role in various aspects of the Market Delivery Operations expansion. I was involved in opening new buildings, recruiting exceptional associates, developing new platform SOPs (Standard Operating Procedures), and leading pilot projects to enhance operations and productivity.

As a high-performing supervisor, I excelled in my role, traveling to multiple locations to assist during their building go-live transitions. I also provided training and guidance to numerous emerging leaders, helping them effectively manage their teams. Additionally, I trained some exceptional associates who went on to become successful leaders in their own right. Over time, I started receiving emails from multiple associates seeking mentorship and guidance.

During this time, my wife and I decided to take a leap of faith and give purchasing our first home another try. Despite being told it was impossible, we were determined to make it happen. I diligently sent all our paperwork to the lender, who then outlined what was needed for approval.

Over the next four months, we worked tirelessly to fix the necessary paperwork, and when we returned to the lender, we finally received our pre-approval and the green light to start house hunting. We eventually found an incredible house that my wife absolutely loved – it was fully finished and perfect for us. In August 2020, we officially became homeowners.

Our journey serves as a reminder not to give up. As James N. Watkins said, "A river cuts through a rock not because of its power but because of its persistence."

My aspiration for growth persisted, and when a position in Long Island, New York became available, I eagerly applied. Unfortunately, I wasn't selected for the role. However, I sought feedback from my manager at the time, determined to refine my skills for future opportunities. Each rejection led me to a better position. What's meant for you will always find its way.

Eventually, I secured a position in New Jersey, eliminating the need for extensive travel to Long Island. This opportunity marked my promotion to an Inventory Control Quality Assurance Operations Manager, overseeing inventory for both the flatbed distribution center and the bulk distribution center. My experience as a Merchandising Execution Team Associate, Sales Associate, Merchandising Assistant Store Manager, and Inventory Captain had uniquely qualified me for this role. I mentioned earlier the importance of seizing opportunities, and you will indeed be thankful for saying, "Yes." In my case, I was able to utilize my skills as a Merchandising and Inventory Captain to work in this role successfully.

This situation reinforced my belief in never turning down an opportunity, as it might be the very experience that opens doors in the near future. Embrace tasks with humility, for they are preparing you for what lies ahead. This role ultimately paved the way for my promotion to manage my own building. I had the privilege of leading a team during a momentous period when we were onboarding a new delivery agent in a live building, a groundbreaking milestone in the history of MDO (Market Delivery Operations). It was the first carrier swap ever done by the company. Simultaneously, I managed a substantial warehouse expansion and oversaw a private fleet of 26 dedicated drivers. It was a challenging task. My performance in transforming the building and enhancing all key performance indicators subsequently earned me another promotion to a regional Delivery Manager position.

It's astonishing to reflect on my journey – the janitor

from McDonald's, who initially doubted himself when starting at Home Depot, was not even qualified to be a cashier, but who had become an integral part of the regional team as a Regional Delivery Manager. As an associate, I used to hear regional team members recount their humble beginnings as cashiers and in merchandising roles. I couldn't believe it back then. Now, I can affirm the same to other associates: believe in yourself, because anything is possible. Back when I was scrubbing toilets, I never saw myself as leadership material. As the legendary American football coach Vince Lombardi once said, "Leaders aren't born, they are made. And they are made just like anything else, through hard work." What is your goal or aspiration? What are you afraid of? Do you have ambitions? Well, hard work and dedication will help you achieve your goal.

Have you ever heard if this quote from motivational author S.L. Parker? "At 211 degrees, water is hot. At 212 degrees, it boils. And with boiling water, comes steam. And with steam, you can power a train." This quote changed my mindset by simplifying success. All you need is one more degree to power your dream, one more degree to graduate, one more degree more to fix your marriage, one more degree to achieve your dream. "You cannot get what you've never had unless you're willing to do what you've never done." From the inspirational book *212° The Extra Degree* by Mac Anderson and Sam Parker.

With this mindset, life had transformed in ways I could never have imagined. The support, guidance, and opportunities provided by Home Depot had not only transformed my career but also enriched my personal life. I am deeply grateful for the doors that opened and the positive impact this had on my overall well-being.

The belief that I embraced throughout my journey, together with perseverance and determination one could achieve greatness, burned even brighter within me. This fire, ignited by the challenges I faced and the successes I achieved, continued to drive me forward. It fueled my desire to reach new heights, constantly pushing myself to learn and grow both personally and professionally.

I understood the significance of my journey and the impact it had on others around me. I aimed to inspire and motivate those who crossed my path, sharing my story as a testament to the power of resilience, hard work, and determination. I wanted others to believe in their own potential and the possibilities that awaited them.

As I reflected on how far I had come, I was filled with a sense of gratitude and fulfillment. Each step I had taken, no matter how small, led me to this point. I knew my adventure was far from over. I was determined to continue challenging myself, seizing new opportunities, and making a positive difference in the lives of those around me.

With the support of Home Depot, my loved ones, and belief in myself, I was ready to embrace the next chapter of my life and career. Confident that with the same dedication and resilience that had brought me thus far, I would continue to achieve greatness and create a future filled with success, happiness, and fulfillment.

Along the way, a recurring question has surfaced: What ignites my motivation? Surprisingly, it doesn't take much. What keeps me motivated? It's quite simple. I faced a tough start, dealing with political turmoil and witnessing serious crimes at a young age. I've overcome many challenges, and I'm grateful to have the chance to answer this question. What motivates me are the small things, like turning on a light switch and having control over the room's lighting. Back where I come from, such a simple action was a privilege I didn't have, and it reminds me of the inequalities in our circumstances. Now, in a new country, these everyday things that many take for granted are what drive my motivation. It's a reminder of the blessings we often don't fully appreciate.

CHAPTER 8

Overcoming Obstacles to Start a Family

Dealing with the Emotional Toll of Infertility

The year following my father's tragic death in the 7.0 magnitude earthquake, I crossed paths with my wife. Little did I know she would become my greatest source of support. As we got to know one another, our bond grew stronger with each passing day. It seemed like she was a divine presence, sent to guide and uplift me during that challenging period.

During those difficult days residing in my apartment, barely able to make ends meet, my wife proved to be an angel in disguise. She selflessly offered her unwavering support and care. I will never forget the moments when she gathered groceries from her parents' fridge, packing them into a small bag so I could sustain myself for the week. Her kindness and generosity sustained me both physically and emotionally.

In those humble acts of providing nourishment, my wife displayed her love and commitment. She became my pillar of strength, standing by my side through the hardships and uncertainties of life. Together, we faced the challenges head-on, and her presence brought a ray of hope and warmth into my world.

In her presence, I found solace and the courage to keep moving forward. Her unyielding support gave me the strength to believe in myself and my ability to overcome adversity. Upon achieving the position of Assistant Store Manager at Home Depot, it felt like the perfect time to propose to my wife. The following year, we ventured into marriage with the little we had, knowing that love was our foundation, and we were determined to build our future together.

We have endured numerous trials and challenges together, but perhaps the greatest test we faced was our infertility journey. After numerous doctor appointments and multiple attempts to conceive, we finally booked a doctor's appointment to investigate what might be going on. Nervously waiting for the doctor after undergoing multiple tests, we were eager to hear the news, hoping for positive and encouraging results. But the doctor's diagnosis was devastating: my wife had stage 4 endometriosis and fibroids blocking her tubes, which required her to undergo two intense surgeries. It was during those years of trying to conceive and witnessing my wife's struggle that I truly understood the depths of her strength and resilience.

I was present during both surgeries. The first one was incredibly intense, my wife almost lost her life. The doctor urgently called us as she wasn't responsive upon waking from the anesthesia. It was an incredibly scary moment, and we continued to pray fervently in that room. My heart ached seeing my wife in such a critical condition, but thankfully, she recovered quickly. The doctor informed us that everything had gone well.

However, a year later, we received devastating news – my wife needed to undergo another surgery. We thought we were done with such procedures, but there was no escaping this one. We made the difficult decision to proceed with the surgery, holding on to our faith and prayers, hoping it would be the last one.

We didn't give up after the surgery and recovery process. Despite the sadness and the darkness that loomed over us, my wife remained determined to overcome this formidable obstacle. Throughout this journey, I found myself in a unique position as a leader and motivator, encouraging others to persevere and reminding them anything is possible. Little did they know that behind my optimistic messages, I also grappled with my own internal battles.

Being a leader does not exempt anyone from personal hardships. There are moments when we yearn to shed the superhero cape and embrace our vulnerabilities as mere mortals. It is crucial to recognize that leaders, just like anyone else, face their share of obstacles. However, despite the darkness that surrounded me, I firmly believed my personal struggles should not define my attitude. Regardless of the challenges I encountered, I remained committed to staying true to myself and maintaining a positive outlook.

Throughout this phase of our marriage, I witnessed the incredible strength and resilience of my wife. Her determination and courage inspired me to keep pushing forward, no matter what. Together, we navigated the complexities of infertility, finding solace and strength in each other's love and support.

While the road was fraught with difficulties, we never lost hope. We knew this did not define us and brighter days would eventually come. Our belief in the power of positivity fueled our spirits, providing us with the strength to endure. In the midst of our personal struggles, we discovered the importance of being authentic leaders, acknowledging our own challenges while still uplifting those around us.

Today, as I reflect upon our journey, I am reminded of the resilience of the human spirit. Our experience taught me that even in the face of hardships, it is possible to find light and strength within ourselves. I am eternally grateful for my wife's unfaltering resolve and for the lessons learned along the way.

Finally, after three years of infertility, in April 2021, we received the most incredible news: my wife was pregnant. The moment I heard the news, my heart swelled with joy. This was the moment we had been patiently waiting years for. Determined to be there every step of the way, I made sure not to miss any doctor's appointments, cherishing each milestone and savoring the anticipation of our little miracle.

In December 2021, our daughter was born. As I held her in my hands, I was overcome with awe and gratitude. It was a testament to the power of faith and the wonders that can unfold against all odds. Despite what the doctors deemed impossible, God worked a miracle in our lives. The joy we experienced in that moment was immeasurable, and it solidified our belief that with divine intervention, anything is possible. The countless days of sadness and crying were over. It was a burden lifted from our shoulders.

As the joy of our first daughter's arrival filled our hearts, a new question arose: Would we be able to expand our family further? This thought lingered in our minds as we brought her home and adjusted to our new family dynamic. Yet, in the depths of our uncertainty, I reassured my wife with unwavering faith. I reminded her that if God had blessed us once, He would do it again in His perfect timing. Little did I know, as those words escaped my lips, my wife was already carrying our second daughter. The miracle continued, surpassing our expectations and filling our lives with even more love and joy.

On the day of our second daughter's C-section, I found myself in the hospital, still in disbelief that I was experiencing this scenario once again, especially after being told it was impossible. However, in January 2023, our second daughter arrived. It was an incredible moment bringing her home and witnessing the excitement and amazement of our firstborn at her new little sister. Our family was growing at a rapid pace, not exactly as we initially imagined, but we counted God's blessings each day, recognizing His great faithfulness in our lives.

I share this message not only to recount the extraordinary blessings we have received, but also to inspire and encourage those who may be facing their own trials and tribulations. It is a reminder to keep pushing forward, hold on to hope, and never give up. Along the way, were voices that declared our dreams impossible. We experienced moments of doubt and discouragement. However, we steadfastly believed that victory was ours, guided by our unwavering faith in God's providence. We learned that with Him, all things are possible.

This narrative was not solely for us to experience and rejoice in. It was meant to serve as a source of motivation for others, a testament to the human spirit and the power of unwavering faith.

So, to you reading this message, may it be a beacon of hope and a reminder that your path, no matter how arduous, is not in vain. Keep moving forward, for your story has the potential to inspire and uplift others. With God by your side, victory is within reach, and every impossibility can be transformed into a glorious reality.

Finding hope and resilience in the face of adversity.

Finding hope and resilience in the face of adversity is a remarkable feat, especially the strenuous encounter of infertility. It is a path filled with uncertainty, heartache, and countless emotional battles. However, within the darkest moments, there is still room for hope to bloom and resilience to take root.

For those who find themselves on this arduous path, it is essential to acknowledge and embrace the emotions that accompany the journey. It is natural to feel a range of emotions, including sadness, frustration, and even anger. These feelings are valid and should not be suppressed. Instead, allow yourself the space to grieve and process these emotions. Seek support from loved ones, join support groups, or consider therapy as a means of filtering through these complex emotions.

It is crucial to cultivate self-care and prioritize your well-being. Take time to engage in activities that bring you joy, whether it be pursuing a hobby, practicing mindfulness and meditation, or simply taking a break from the constant focus on fertility. Nurturing your physical, mental, and emotional health will not only benefit you but also contribute to a more positive mindset and resilience when facing tough times.

Educating yourself about infertility, treatment options, and available resources can also help with maintaining hope and knowing fully what's going on with a sense of empowerment. Stay informed, ask questions, and engage with healthcare professionals who specialize in infertility. Understanding the process and being an active participant in your own care can foster a sense of control and hope.

In the midst of the ups and downs, remember you are not alone. Reach out to others who have experienced or are currently going through infertility. Connecting with individuals who understand firsthand what you are going through can provide solace, support, and a sense of belonging. Sharing experiences, exchanging advice, and leaning on one another during difficult times can be incredibly powerful.

While the road may seem long and challenging, maintaining a positive outlook can make a significant difference. Cultivate optimism and hope, even when faced with setbacks. Celebrate even the smallest victories and milestones along the way. Remind yourself that you are strong, resilient, and capable of navigating this journey.

Lastly, never underestimate the power of perseverance and the possibility of miracles. Miracles do happen, and they can manifest in unexpected ways. Stay open to alternative paths, treatment options, or even the idea of building a family through other means such as adoption or surrogacy. There are different paths to parenthood, and each one is equally valid and beautiful.

In the midst of the pain, frustration, and uncertainty, hold onto hope. Infertility is a formidable challenge, but it does not define your worth or diminish your capacity for joy and love. Embrace the journey with courage, compassion for yourself, and an unwavering belief that hope will prevail.

God was the cornerstone of our journey, the guiding force that sustained us through the storm. Along the way, we encountered countless individuals who, perhaps unknowingly, inquired about our plans for starting a family. This added an additional layer of pain to our already tough situation. Despite these thoughtless remarks, we remained steadfast in our faith, relying on each other and God as our anchor.

Through the trials and tribulations, we learned the true

essence of marriage—a sacred bond that transcends circumstances and requires unwavering support for one another. As we stood at the altar, reciting our wedding vows, we understood that marriage is not solely about sharing joyous moments but also enduring tough times together, hand-in-hand.

In moments of uncertainty and heartache, we clung to our commitment to each other and our faith. We found solace in knowing we were not alone. With God by our side, we drew strength from His love and guidance, trusting that His plan for us would unfold in due time.

Going through infertility taught us the values of patience and empathy. We became acutely aware of the impact our words and actions can have on others, vowing to treat others with kindness and respect, even when we may not understand their struggles.

In the end, it was our relentless belief in God's plan that carried us through. We learned to surrender our desires and place our trust in Him, knowing His timing is perfect. Our faith reminded us there is beauty in the midst of adversity and miracles can manifest in unexpected ways.

So, if you are facing a similar journey, remember that your marriage is not defined by the ability to conceive but by the love, support, and commitment you share. Lean on each other, seek solace in your faith, and remain open to the blessings that may come your way. May your love and reliance on God be the bedrock that sustains you through the trials, and may your journey ultimately lead you to a place of joy, whether through the gift of children or in embracing a different path that unfolds before you.

CHAPTER 9

Gratitude and Reflection
―――――――――――

Reflecting on the Journey and the Lessons Learned

Reflecting on my journey, I have gained invaluable insights and wisdom. From the moment of my birth, when I overcame the challenges of a difficult delivery and the skepticism of the nurses, it should have been evident resilience would be my greatest asset. This trait would carry me through the various obstacles and trials that awaited me.

I have experienced the highs and lows of life, from navigating unfamiliar territories in a foreign country to grieving the loss of certain dreams and infertility. During my upbringing, my parents did their best to raise my sister and me with the limited resources available to them. At one point, our financial situation was so challenged, I vividly recall this particular incident. My mom purchased a pair of sneakers for me, but one shoe had a hole in the front. I sat in the living room, observing my mom meticulously sewing it back together, ensuring it would last me another year. While other kids excitedly showcased their new shoes, I prepared to visit the shoe fixer to have the sole reattached. Over time, the shoes lost their original shape. I also had to be cautious not to dirty my uniform since I didn't have enough pants to last the entire week.

We even resorted to using a charcoal iron to press our uniforms due to the lack of electricity.

These events taught me about resilience, appreciating what I have, and making the most of challenging circumstances. Despite the financial hardships, my parents' determination and resourcefulness allowed us to persevere. Material possessions may not define our worth, but the strength and love within our family were priceless.

Despite experiencing moments of despair, including sleeping in a basement, I never allowed those circumstances to shape my identity. Instead, I summoned my inner strength and determination to overcome hard times. Through increased perseverance, I exchanged sleeping on cardboard in a basement for becoming a proud homeowner. This personal triumph stands as a testament to my tenacity and refusal to be defined by my past.

Moreover, I have also experienced substantial growth and achievements in my professional life. I've dedicated myself to developing my skills and seizing opportunities, allowing me to reach new heights and accomplish noteworthy goals. These professional accomplishments further validate my commitment to personal growth and success.

Through it all, I have learned that life is a blend of victories and defeats. It is important to cultivate resilience during difficult times and celebrate every achievement, no matter how big or small. It is crucial not to let our goals blind us to the joy of the present moment. We must adopt gratitude and appreciate each step of our journey.

Never doubt your own worth and potential. Others' opinions of you should never shape your reality. It is vital to fight for what you want and make your own way. Remember that you are the creator of your own destiny.

During moments of darkness, it is essential to recognize we are not buried but planted. These challenging times are not meant to harm us, but rather to strengthen us. Just as the roots of a tree grow deeper in darkness, so too do we find inner strength and resilience during our most trying moments.

I often draw parallels between my life and the transformative process of a caterpillar. Like a caterpillar destined to become a butterfly, I have undergone my own metamorphosis. This shift may have been filled with darkness and uncertainty, much like the caterpillar inside its chrysalis. However, just as the caterpillar emerges from its cocoon, ready to explore the world and fulfill its purpose, I too have emerged stronger and more determined to welcome life's possibilities.

Recognizing that I had complete control over my life, I faced crucial decisions that would shape my path. Despite being surrounded by drug violence in Coney Island, I had to choose whether I would succumb to negative influences or rise above them. I contemplated whether I would become entangled in the system, potentially acquiring a criminal record and facing incarceration. However, I held deep respect for the values instilled in me by my parents, particularly my father's teachings about honoring our family's last name. It was this reverence that guided my choices and prevented me from engaging in reckless behavior.

Throughout the pages of this book, I have emphasized a valuable lesson: whatever challenges you may be facing, are merely temporary stops along your journey, not your ultimate destination. I draw upon an analogy that resonates deeply with me—the train rides I used to take in Coney Island. I vividly recall the voice over the loudspeaker announcing, "This is a Manhattan-bound train, next stop is Brighton Beach. Stand clear of the closing door, please." It struck me that we don't disembark at a station with no relevance to our intended destination. Similarly, in life, we must remain focused and resolute, standing firmly as the doors close, because we are enroute to our desired outcome.

Finding gratitude and hope for the future.

I have discovered the incredible kindness and authenticity that resides in people's hearts. Take, for instance, the supervisor I mentioned earlier who generously gifted me $600—an act for which I will be eternally grateful. On a memorable occasion when I was asked to deliver a speech, he happened to be present, allowing me to publicly acknowledge him by name for the tremendous impact he had on my life. During a period when I was on the verge of giving up, his support reignited my fire which has been burning brightly ever since.

The Home Depot's company culture has played a significant role in guiding me through both my professional and personal life. It was within that environment I honed my leadership skills and gained a profound understanding of how to effectively connect with others. In a testament to their commitment, the company even visited my home to create a short documentary that captured the essence of my journey—the driving force behind my determination and ultimate success.

It is essential to recognize that claiming sole credit for my achievements would be the greatest falsehood. Above all, I owe my transformation to God's grace, the unwavering support of my wife and newfound family, and the multiple leaders who invested in me. Their valuable advice has guided me in both my professional and personal endeavors. Navigating life's obstacles cannot be undertaken alone; it necessitates the support and guidance of others.

My wife's situation encouraged a new drive within me to strive for greatness. Her perseverance is unparalleled, especially in her pursuit of expanding our family and bringing two beautiful daughters into the world. Witnessing her strength, even as she lay on the operating table, bleeding, while I held our babies in my hands, is a feeling words cannot adequately express. In the recovery room, despite her pain, she selflessly urged me to get some rest, even though she needed it more than anyone.

During her second pregnancy, I made the decision to re-enroll in college, a path I had veered away from years ago due to financial and life circumstances. It was my wife's encouragement that prompted my return to school. As I began my final semester, coinciding with the birth of our second daughter, I faced a critical moment. While in the recovery room, as much as I wanted to abandon my classes, I drew strength from my wife's ability to rise above the challenges. Holding my newborn daughter in the middle of the night, while my wife recovered from a C-section, I realized that if she could summon the strength to care for our child, I could persevere in my studies. And so, I pressed on.

Amidst the whirlwind of adjusting to fatherhood, I diligently completed my assignments from the hospital room. Months later, I walked across the stage, graduating from college. It was a momentous occasion, as it marked my very first graduation ceremony since I had not participated in my high school graduation. This time, however, I had a purpose.

I recorded the moment, capturing photos and videos, ensuring that my new family could witness and celebrate this achievement. The relief and sense of accomplishment that washed over me as I held my diploma in my hands were indescribable. Although it took me over a decade to achieve this milestone, I learned that it's not about how you start, but how you finish. A diploma has no expiration date. It's never too late to revisit your dreams and pick up where you left off.

My daughters' growth has imparted valuable lessons to me as well. Witnessing their journey from crawling to walking and now running around our home, and hearing their babbling turn into their first words, to now saying "Daddy," I have come to realize the significance of taking baby steps in life. In order to run, one must first learn to crawl, and in order to speak, one must first babble. This principle of life applies to every aspect of our existence.

If you find yourself in the early stages of crawling, there is no need to worry. Walking and running will inevitably follow. If you are already running, be assured there is always room for a smoother stride and a quicker time. Just as climbing comes after running, there are new heights to reach and challenges to conquer. Life is an ongoing journey of continuous improvement, and each step forward brings us closer to our fullest potential.

Embrace the process, no matter where you are on your path. Celebrate the small victories and have faith that with persistence and dedication, you will continue to evolve and achieve greater things. Remember that life's lessons can be found in the simplest acts, and the progress you make today will lay the foundation for the achievements of tomorrow. Keep moving forward, for there is always room to improve and thrive in life's remarkable journey.

Every year, it has become a tradition for me to visit the McDonald's where I once worked as a janitor. This annual pilgrimage is not just a nostalgic trip; it's a profound source of motivation that reminds me of my humble beginnings and the incredible journey I've embarked on since then.

As I step into that McDonald's, I can still vividly recall the days when I diligently cleaned floors and kept the place tidy. Those moments of hard work and dedication laid the foundation for the resilience and determination I carry with me today. It's a reminder that success is a journey, and it's essential never to forget where you started.

But the journey doesn't stop there. After my visit to McDonald's, I take a drive down the road to the supermarket where I once worked as a cashier. This place symbolizes the belief that nothing is impossible. It serves as a testament to the boundless opportunities that await those who are willing to work hard and chase their dreams.

Seeing that supermarket reminds me that I am the author of my own story, and my past does not define my future. It's a place where I exchanged groceries for smiles and customer service excellence. It's proof that with dedication, perseverance, and a strong work ethic, we can turn our aspirations into reality.

CHAPTER 10

Six Steps to Change Your Circumstances and Become *UNBREAKABLE*

_____

"Discover the Path to Change Your Circumstances and Cultivate Unbreakable Resilience"

The essential awareness that the decision to undertake change begins with a firm choice to move away from one's current circumstances is at the core of human growth and transformation. The phrase "The first step towards getting somewhere is to decide that you are not going to stay where you are" perfectly describes this revolutionary period.

Imagine yourself at a crossroads in life when there is doubt about the way forward. This quotation serves as a helpful reminder that all types of achievement—including change—require a deliberate modification in viewpoint. It conveys a strong understanding that giving in to complacency and stagnation would not help one achieve their goals. One must be willing to face the discomfort of letting go of the comfortable and muster the bravery to change directions in order to develop.

This choice to move forward from where you are right now is a call to action. It's the emergence of a proactive attitude that recognizes the necessity for development and advancement. This choice sets you in motion, encouraging you to venture into unfamiliar territory, make important goals, and relentlessly work toward accomplishing them.

The remark also highlights the importance of personal agency in determining one's future. It acknowledges that you are the source of the first spark of transformation and puts the power firmly in your hands. This critical decision-making process necessitates reflection, self-awareness, and a readiness to accept change.

This decision is not without difficulties, though. Leaving your comfort zone might be frightening since it frequently requires conquering challenges, facing uncertainty, and putting up with discomfort. But the magic actually happens right here. You can enter a world of opportunities, progress, and fulfillment by accepting change and refusing to settle.

In essence, "The first step towards getting somewhere is to decide that you are not going to stay where you are" embodies the philosophy of continuous improvement. It exhorts you to take charge of your fate, pursue professional and personal growth, and welcome fresh starts with open arms. It serves as a powerful reminder that every great journey begins with a single, deliberate choice to embark on a path of transformation and progress. I'm going to share with you six steps that helped me change my circumstances and become *Unbreakable*. Perhaps they will work for you, too.

-1-
Evaluate Your Current Situation

Taking an honest look at my current circumstances was an essential step towards initiating change in my life. I recognized the areas that required improvement, such as my career, relationships, health, or personal development. By honestly assessing where I stood, I created a clear vision of where I wanted to go and what I wanted to achieve.

I understood that struggles and challenges were not permanent roadblocks but temporary hurdles that could lead to something greater. I shifted my perspective, viewing obstacles as opportunities to tap into my full potential. Being open to challenges and working through them enabled me to change the course of my life and progress towards my desired outcomes.

I've had to constantly remind myself that obstacles were not meant to hold me back; they were meant to propel me forward. Each hurdle provided valuable lessons, shaped my character, and helped me reach new heights. I came to understand that what truly mattered was not how my life started, but the progress I made along the way.

Taking responsibility for my life was an empowering realization. Instead of blaming external factors or other people, I recognized that I had the power to shape my own destiny. By accepting accountability, I reclaimed control over my life and opened doors to personal growth and development.

It was common for me to attribute life situations to external factors like parents, God, and my environment, however this perspective limited my potential. I embraced the understanding that my unique life's path led me to understand my true potential and inspire others. By accepting my circumstances and leveraging them as opportunities for growth, I harnessed my abilities to make a positive impact on myself and those around me.

Through honestly assessing my current circumstances, embracing challenges, taking responsibility for my life, and recognizing the potential for growth, I transformed my trajectory and moved closer to my desired outcomes. I understood that obstacles were not roadblocks but steppingstones towards personal progress and reaching new heights. My advice to others is to bravely confront your current circumstances, acknowledge areas that need improvement, and embrace challenges as opportunities for growth. Take responsibility for your life and recognize the power you have to shape your future. By doing so, you can unlock your true potential and make a positive impact on your journey towards achieving your desired outcomes.

-2-
Set Clear Goals

In my pursuit of success, I discovered that establishing specific, measurable, and realistic goals was vital. These goals needed to align with the changes I wanted to bring into my life, serving as guiding principles that provided direction and purpose. However, I soon realized setting broad goals alone wouldn't suffice. I needed to break them down into smaller, actionable steps to make tangible progress. These steps became the building blocks of my transformation, each one concrete, time-bound, and manageable, allowing me to consistently work towards my desired outcome.

By defining clear goals and breaking them down into actionable steps, I created a roadmap that not only provided structure but also fueled my motivation. As I accomplished each step, no matter how small, I experienced a sense of achievement that propelled me forward with renewed enthusiasm and determination. Celebrations of my successes became crucial as they served as powerful motivators and reminders of my progress.

Regularly monitoring my progress, tracking milestones, and reflecting on my journey allowed me to adjust my strategies, learn from setbacks, and make necessary course corrections.

Throughout this process, I embraced the understanding that change is a journey. Clear goals kept me focused, resilient, and driven. They provided the framework for my actions and ensured that I stayed on track towards my desired outcomes. By harnessing the transformative power of setting clear, measurable, and realistic goals, I was able to witness significant strides towards the changes I aspired to achieve in my life.

-3-

Develop a Growth Mindset

Developing a growth mindset has been instrumental for me personally and professionally. I strongly advise you to embrace this mindset as well. It begins with cultivating a belief that our abilities, intelligence, and skills can be developed through dedication, effort, and continuous learning. By adopting a growth mindset, we come to understand challenges are not roadblocks, but rather opportunities for improvement and growth. Viewing setbacks and failures as valuable lessons allows us to gain insights and propel ourselves towards success.

With a growth mindset, we approach obstacles with a positive attitude, knowing that we have the capacity to overcome them. It is essential to embark on a lifelong journey of self-improvement, constantly seeking new knowledge, acquiring skills, and gaining diverse experiences. This mindset enables us to unlock our true potential by pushing beyond our comfort zones and achieving remarkable growth and accomplishments that may have once seemed unattainable.

To develop a growth mindset, it is necessary to cultivate a positive attitude towards our own abilities and potential. We must foster a belief that with the right strategies, hard work, and perseverance, we can overcome obstacles and achieve our goals. Approaching tasks with enthusiasm and actively seeking ways to stretch our abilities and expand our knowledge are key elements in this process.

Continuous learning becomes the foundation of our growth mindset. We should actively seek opportunities to acquire new skills, knowledge, and experiences. Embracing feedback as a valuable tool for growth and viewing criticism as an opportunity to learn and improve are essential practices. Surrounding ourselves with like-minded individuals who inspire and support our growth journey also contributes significantly to our development.

Cultivating resilience and perseverance is another vital aspect of developing a growth mindset. Understanding that progress often comes with setbacks and challenges, we must remain resilient in the face of adversity. Rather than being discouraged, we can use these moments as opportunities to develop our problem-solving skills and emotional fortitude.

-4-
Take Action

When it comes to achieving success, taking consistent and focused action towards your goals is paramount. It's important to understand that progress is not always immediate or dramatic but rather a gradual process. By starting with small steps, you lay the foundation for larger accomplishments and build momentum along the way. Each small action serves as a building block, propelling you forward and instilling a sense of confidence in your abilities.

Staying committed and disciplined is essential, especially during challenging times or when faced with setbacks. It's natural to encounter moments of self-doubt or procrastination, but it's essential not to let those moments hinder your progress. Instead, acknowledge those feelings and fears, but don't allow them to dictate your actions. Take that leap of faith, even if it means stepping outside of your comfort zone, and you'll discover that the act of taking action itself can be transformative.

Embrace the opportunity to challenge yourself and push beyond what you thought was possible. By taking consistent and focused action, you can break through the barriers of self-limiting beliefs and prove to yourself that you are capable of far more than you initially believed. Each step forward becomes an opening for forward momentum.

Persistence is key. No matter what obstacles you encounter along the way, maintain a determined mindset and keep moving forward. Celebrate your progress, no matter how small, and use it as fuel to propel you towards your ultimate goals. Trust in yourself and your abilities, knowing that each action you take brings you closer to the future you desire.

-5-
Seek Support and Surround Yourself with Positive Influences

Surrounding myself with people who supported and encouraged my trajectory of change played a significant role in my transformation. Their belief in my potential and their constant support provided the necessary encouragement and motivation I needed to stay committed to my goals. These individuals became my pillars of strength, offering guidance, empathy, and encouragement during times of doubt or challenges.

I actively sought out mentors and coaches who had expertise and experience in the areas I wanted to improve. Their guidance and insights were truly life changing. They shared valuable perspectives, offered practical tools, and shared strategies to navigate obstacles and overcome challenges. Their wisdom and experience became a compass that helped me chart my course, avoiding common pitfalls and making more informed decisions. Through their mentorship, I gained clarity, refined my strategies, and accelerated my progress towards my desired outcomes.

Engaging in communities and groups with similar goals and interests allowed me to connect with like-minded individuals who were also on personal growth journeys. Together, we formed a network of support where we shared our experiences, challenges, and triumphs. The sense of camaraderie and understanding within these communities was invaluable. We inspired and motivated one another, celebrated each other's milestones, and provided a safe space to share our struggles and seek advice. Being part of such a community created a sense of belonging and fostered an environment of progress.

Surrounding myself with positive influences also served as a form of accountability. Being in the company of individuals who believed in my abilities and goals motivated me to stay focused, disciplined, and consistent in my efforts. Their unwavering support fueled my determination to push myself beyond my comfort zones, take calculated risks, and strive for greatness. Their belief in me became a source of inspiration, encouraging me to step into my full potential and embrace the challenges that came my way.

-6-
Practice Resilience

Cultivating resilience has been a crucial aspect of my personal growth and ability to work through challenges and setbacks. I have learned that life is full of unexpected twists and turns, our resilience determines how we respond to these obstacles. Resilience is not about avoiding difficulties or pretending that everything is always perfect; it is about developing the inner strength and strategies to bounce back from setbacks and maintain a positive outlook.

One of the key strategies I have found effective in building resilience is to focus on developing emotional strength and adaptability. This involves recognizing and acknowledging my emotions, allowing myself to feel and process them, and then finding healthy ways to cope and move forward. It's important to remember that it's okay to experience a range of emotions when faced with challenges, but it's how we respond and bounce back that truly matters.

Seeking lessons and growth opportunities in every obstacle has also been instrumental in my resilience journey. Instead of viewing setbacks as failures or roadblocks, I choose to see them as valuable learning experiences. Every challenge presents an opportunity for growth, self-reflection, and self-improvement. By adopting this mindset, I am able to extract wisdom and knowledge from even the most difficult situations, ultimately helping me become stronger and more resilient.

Building resilience requires a proactive approach. It involves developing a toolbox of coping strategies and self-care practices that work for you. This may include activities such as mindfulness, exercise, journaling, connecting with loved ones, or seeking professional support when needed. Experiment with different techniques and find what resonates with you the most. Regularly engage in these practices to build your emotional resilience and maintain a positive mindset.
Finally, it's important to remember that resilience is not

a fixed trait but something that can be developed and strengthened over time. It requires consistent effort, self-reflection, and a commitment to personal growth. Embrace challenges as opportunities to build your resilience muscle, knowing that each time you overcome an obstacle, you become unbreakable in the face of adversity.

Looking back on my journey, one piece of advice I would offer to others on becoming unbreakable is to develop a strong sense of self-belief and confidence. Embrace your strengths, talents, and capabilities, and recognize that you have the power within you to overcome any challenge. Trust in your abilities and remember that you have successfully overcome obstacles in the past, which proves your resilience. Surround yourself with positive influences and supportive individuals who believe in you and uplift your spirits. Additionally, practice self-care and prioritize your well-being, as it plays a vital role in maintaining your mental and emotional resilience. Finally, adopt a growth mindset and view setbacks as learning opportunities that propel you forward. With determination, perseverance, and a positive mindset, you can cultivate unbreakability and face any adversity that comes your way. Remember, you are stronger than you think, and with each challenge, you have the opportunity to become even more unbreakable.

To be unbreakable is to possess a resilience that can withstand the harshest circumstances. It's like the mighty oak tree that stands tall amidst fierce storms, its roots firmly grounded in the earth. Despite the strong winds, the tree bends and sways, but it never breaks. In the same way, being unbreakable is akin to a diamond, formed under immense pressure and heat. It remains unyielding, radiating brilliance even in the most challenging conditions.

Being unbreakable goes beyond mere endurance—it encompasses the ability to face hardships and challenges with unwavering hope and without compromising your core values. It means adapting to adversity, finding solutions, and emerging stronger than before. Just as the oak tree and diamond exemplify, your spirit remains unshattered, and your determination remains unwavering, regardless of the circumstances.

To cultivate unbreakability, develop a resilient mindset

that views obstacles as opportunities for growth. Embrace challenges as catalysts for personal development and learn from each experience. Nurture a strong sense of self-belief, knowing that you have the strength within you to overcome any adversity. Surround yourself with a supportive network of individuals who uplift and inspire you.

Practice self-care and prioritize your mental and emotional well-being. Cultivate habits that enhance your resilience, such as practicing gratitude, engaging in regular exercise, and maintaining healthy relationships. Remember…setbacks are not failures but steppingstones on the path to success. Stay focused, persevere through difficulties, and maintain an unwavering belief in your ability to overcome.

In conclusion, being unbreakable means embodying a steadfast resilience that can weather the storms of life. Like the oak tree and diamond, you have the capacity to adapt, overcome, and emerge stronger from challenges. Hold onto your core values, maintain hope, and never let circumstances break your spirit or diminish your resolve.

By embracing this unbreakable mindset, you can navigate through life's trials with grace and emerge triumphant.

KEEP IN TOUCH!

www.kevinmarius.com

www.ingramcontent.com/pod-product-compliance
Lightning Source LLC
LaVergne TN
LVHW091255080426
835510LV00007B/271